the No Spin zone

CONFRONTATIONS WITH THE

POWERFUL AND FAMOUS IN AMERICA

BILL O'REILLY

AFTERWORD BY JAMES ELLROY

BROADWAY BOOKS | New York

the No Spin zone

A hardcover edition of this book was published in 2001 by Broadway Books.

THE NO SPIN ZONE. Copyright © 2001 by Bill O'Reilly. All rights reserved. No part of this book may be reproduced or transmitted in any form or by any means, electronic or mechanical, including photocopying, recording, or by any information storage and retrieval system, without written permission from the publisher. For information, address Broadway Books, a division of Random House, Inc.

PRINTED IN THE UNITED STATES OF AMERICA

BROADWAY BOOKS and its logo, a letter B bisected on the diagonal, are trademarks of Random House, Inc.

Visit our website at www.broadwaybooks.com

First trade paperback edition published 2003

The Library of Congress has cataloged the hardcover edition as follows:

O'Reilly, Bill.
  The no spin zone: confrontations with the rich and powerful in America / Bill O'Reilly.
    p.   cm.
  1. United States—Politics and government—2001- 2. United States—Politics and government—1993–2001. 3. United States—Social conditions—1980- 4. Politicians—United States—Interviews. 5. Celebrities—United States—Interviews. 6. O'Reilly, Bill—Political and social views. I. Title.

E902.O74 2001b
973.92—dc21

2001043031

ISBN 0-7679-0849-X

10 9 8 7

FOR MAUREEN, FOREVER

"For the haughty men
have risen up against me,
the ruthless seek my life."

—PSALM 54:3

"A man flattened by an opponent
can get up again.
A man flattened by conformity
stays down for good."

—THOMAS WATSON, JR.

contents

the No Spin zone

Opening Bell

This is it . . . we're on live in the No Spin Zone. It's a nightmare place for charlatans and deceivers. But it's a great place for you and everybody else who believes in truth, common sense, and decency.

In the No Spin Zone you can watch those charlatans stammer and the spinners slip out in shame. See, this is a place I've set up over my years of TV interviewing with a special set of purposes: In the No Spin Zone rationalizations are scorned, lies are rejected, and equivocations are mocked. It's a place where quite a few smirks have turned to frowns.

To anybody who uses power and fame to exploit the less powerful, the Zone is a very dangerous place. On the other side, the Zone is comforting to those who live life with a sense of fairness, for it is a place where truth is sought without regret. When Ernest Hemingway decided to write stories that spotlighted the harsh truth alive in this world, he said anybody trying to do that better have a built-in bull detector. I believe I inherited this device from my late father, who would walk out of the room if you couldn't make your point in sixty seconds.

Is the No Spin Zone needed? Well, here's how bad things have gotten in America. The Josephson Institute of Ethics reports that nearly half of all high school students steal. Seven in ten admit to cheating on tests, and 92 percent say they lie. And most of those kids don't feel much guilt at all. Remorse is becoming obsolete in the USA. Excuses cover all misdeeds. After all, there is a disease to cover just about every immoral action, and if you question that, you are a mean, insensitive person. The misery industry has it all covered.

What caused this deplorable state of affairs? Number one, "cowardly parenting." Number two, "corrupt national leadership." As the tree is bent, so it will grow. And today kids can look all around at so many bent adults that they can hardly guess what it means to be straight. People basking in the spotlight—and I don't mean just politicians—are forever presenting terrible examples to the children of America.

Public misbehavior by the famous is a powerful teaching tool. For example, any wide-awake youngster knows that you can make a handsome living in America by being able to spin the truth—that is, twisting the facts of a troubling situation until it is impossible to figure out what the hell is going on. In the CIA it is called disinformation. In the world of politics, show business, finance, and the law it's simply called spin.

Certain immoral acts can be chalked up to "gaining experience." Ever heard of any famous person's "youthful indiscretions"? "Experiments" with illegal drugs? Someone caught driving under the influence is, in my No Spin Zone, a criminal. But with a highly paid lawyer's spin, there is no crime, there is only a "chemical dependence." Even the slowest of children pick up these "lessons" very quickly. (By the way, it is hard to argue with Washington, D.C., based psychiatrist Dr. Sally Satel, who argues that labeling addiction "a chronic, relapsing brain disease . . . gives everybody a pass.")

Criminals don't commit crimes; they "make mistakes." And often it is society's fault that those "mistakes" even happened in the first place. At the end of the day, every child has learned the Lesson of Spin: Almost every wrong action can be stripped of consequences, along with the need for feelings of guilt and remorse.

It all ends nicely. The wrongdoer walks and maybe even prospers from his problems (Robert Downey, Jr., landed a plum role on *Ally McBeal*). The lawyer earns his dough, and sometimes the media benefit from increased reader- and viewership. The show must go on.

But this is wrong.

"Where there is no vision, the people perish," wrote King Solomon in Proverbs more than two millennia ago. When there is no public morality, the nation loses its way.

Who quoted Solomon's words in his acceptance of the nomination of his party as presidential candidate in 1992? Hint: It wasn't George Herbert Walker Bush. No. The man echoing Solomon's warnings about public morality was William Jefferson Clinton.

How ironic it is that Mr. Clinton and his cohorts during impeachment gave America the most effective lessons in the history of this country of what spin can do. Armies of well-paid men and women marched into the living rooms of America via television weaving blankets of deceit for Bill Clinton. "It's just about sex," they wailed. "Everybody lies about sex." "It's a right-wing conspiracy!" "It doesn't rise to the level of impeachment!" and on and on.

The president himself set a terrific example by lying outright to the nation on national television. None of this, of course, was lost on the kids who, according to a variety of surveys, are lying like crazy and have now embraced oral sex with, you might say, presidential abandon.

Mr. Clinton's excellent spin adventure turned out to be just the beginning of the Empire of Spin. The presidential election of 2000 turned out to be a swamp of distortion, diversion, and brazen deception. Both sides presented unprincipled mouthpieces to utter exhausting, incomprehensible bilge. And much of the press in America readily accepted all the garbage without analysis or reflection. After all, it's too difficult and dangerous to challenge those in authority. The cocktail party invitations may stop coming.

We live, finally, in a just world, so maybe that's why the results were so close and why about half of those eligible to vote didn't even show up. I'm not spinning for them—they let their country down—but the exit polls showed that less than 20 percent of Americans were enthusiastic about their vote. Most of us voted for the lesser of two spinners.

The kinds of things I've mentioned are not trivial to me. They have driven me to disgust and near despair in recent years. That is exactly why I created the No Spin Zone on my TV program *The O'Reilly Factor*.

The Zone is open to anyone. I mean that. We invite all newsmakers to come and chat with us. If you don't see certain people there who are hot in the news, that's probably because *they* refuse to enter the Zone of No Spin. Al Gore would not get his passport stamped. Ditto the new junior senator from New York, and former presidential hopeful Elizabeth Dole, and Bob Jones III, president of the notorious Bob Jones University, down in South Carolina. Perhaps the most famous no spin no-show of all is Jesse Jackson. We investigated his finances for a year before cracking the case wide open. Jackson spun the tax-exempt payments to mistress Karin Stanford as "omissions" on the tax returns of one of his foundations. Sure, Jesse.

Celebrities from other worlds, especially actors and actresses, shy away from the Zone too. As you probably know, practically any magazine "interview" you read has been carefully controlled by the star's publicist. Editors and writers agree to avoid touchy issues; otherwise they could lose access to other celebrities handled by the same publicist. When you see a famous person walk into the No Spin Zone, no such bargain has been struck. There are never preconditions for an interview.

Some who don't like the Zone spin it as a place where rude questions are asked. That is nonsense. All I ask is for powerful people to respond honestly to the questions, and if they can't, explain why. The Fifth Amendment is alive in the Zone, but if you take it, be prepared to explain *why* you are taking it.

The children of America have seen with their own eyes that liars can win and cheaters can prosper. They know that our nation will accept venal behavior and, in some cases, reward it with tremendous wealth and power. So why shouldn't they lie, cheat, and steal? After all, it is now part of the culture. After all, the president was caught lying—and he walked.

The antidote to this is some no spin news about people who reject bad behavior. Derek Jeter, the spectacular New York Yankees shortstop, recently signed a huge ten-year contract. Jeter seems to be an honest, hardworking guy and thus a good role model for kids. When asked if that would change now that he makes megamillions and if the money would go to his head, Jeter opined: "No chance. My dad would kill me."

A no spin parent. We need millions more of them.

✳

In hopes of kicking the living daylights out of the spin that has become part of our national dialogue, I've brought together sixteen turbocharged chapters about the most intense issues of the day. We'll discuss problems like teen sex, inappropriate gay activism, the exploitation of working Americans, and raunchy entertainment. I have chosen topics that I believe are extremely relevant to our daily lives.

In each chapter you hear two sides: mine and the opinion of someone who's deeply involved with the issue we are talking about. These debates are taken from interviews I've conducted during my twenty-seven years in broadcast journalism. The interviews are only edited to leave out the uhs, duhs, uh-ohs, and are-you-kidding-mes, many of which are mine. Printing all the equivocation verbatim would drive you nuts—so I just get to the "pith" of the interview, as is my wont.

In each of these chapters you are the final judge of who has the strongest argument. Because it's my book, I get to set things up with commentary, and that may be a bit unfair, but hey, it *is* my book.

These pages do not try to persuade you to believe a certain way. I *am* trying to set forth some insights, some solutions, and some perspective on the most vexing problems of the day. You'll let me know if I succeed.

Each chapter stands alone. You may find yourself browsing

back and forth, depending on what subject or personality catches your eye on a particular day. Also, I've chosen some interviews that are like verbal boxing matches. Who jabs with the stronger argument? Who gets knocked down verbally? You be the judge.

Will George W. Bush's arguments with me on the death penalty stand up or get flattened? What about Al Sharpton's provocations on race, or Susan Sarandon's charges of police racism in New York City? And as I've been asking for years: How does Jesse Jackson get all those millions of dollars?

So settle in and don't be squeamish. You are keeping the score at all times. There is usually a loser in the No Spin Zone and sometimes it's me. But sympathy is not in play. We are chasing down the truth here and that is a hard game. Enjoy the book.

CHAPTER ONE

"You Kidding Me?"

ISSUE 1: Sexual deviants who prey on children
THE OPPONENT: Floyd Abrams, First Amendment attorney

O'REILLY: This doesn't have anything to do with free speech.
ABRAMS: But of course it does.
O'REILLY: No, this has to do with aiding and abetting, promoting a crime on a website.

If you are thirty-five or older, chances are good that your childhood in America was pretty much like mine, no matter where you grew up. By age six I was out of the house most of the time after school and all during the summer, playing with my tight group of friends. There were limits. For example, if I was late for dinner at six o'clock, there was hell to pay.

Otherwise I was on my own in the great outdoors. My parents

seemingly had no fear that I would be harmed by sinister outside forces marauding around my Long Island neighborhood. Sure, I might hurt myself roughhousing, but hey, those were the breaks. My father didn't sound like football announcer John Madden, but he had Madden's mind-set: "Play rough—take your chances."

With my dopey friends, whom you might have met in my last book, *The O'Reilly Factor*, I made the most of the deep woods three blocks from my house. We climbed thirty feet up into the thick leafy branches to build rickety tree houses. We tunneled underground like moles. We threw rocks at each other. We rolled around in the dirt completely unsupervised by annoying adults.

It never occurred to us that some older guy in an overcoat might drive up and try to hurt us. Yes, my father once said something about never taking a ride with a stranger. But he didn't say why, didn't make an issue out of it, and didn't seem concerned that his eldest son might be taken hostage at some point.

How times have changed. And that's the terrifying subject of this chapter's debate with a distinguished First Amendment lawyer and public figure, who I believe is absolutely wrong in putting the rights of special (read perverted) interests ahead of the safety of American children.

Parents today are rightfully worried about their children being abducted or abused, even in their own neighborhoods. But why is that? Are there more child molesters in the United States now than in my childhood years in the fifties and sixties? Are they bolder for some reason? Is it possible they are being encouraged?

Statistically, it is impossible to know. Officials at the FBI and the Department of Health and Human Services say they do not have accurate statistics for child abuse and abduction before 1990. According to the federal government, more than 100,000 American kids were sexually molested in 1998, or one and a half children per one thousand. In 1999 nearly 32,000 kids were kidnapped—most by relatives. England does a better job of tracking the danger-to-kids trend. Scotland Yard says the number of convictions for gross indecency with a child doubled between 1985 and 1995. So the data suggest that society has become more menacing to children and that more adults are willing to risk imprisonment and social destruction to molest kids. The question is why?

Some believe that widespread, often-hysterical TV coverage has possibly encouraged deviant behavior toward children. Because of television news, crimes against children have been magnified greatly. The heartbreak of any child damaged by an adult is spread from coast to coast immediately and the experts start prattling, some of them sympathetic to the "disease" or "condition" of the victimizer. No one can say for sure, but the notoriety of the crimes may attract pedophiles who are risk takers. We are obviously not talking about rational people here.

But there is also something else in play in this country that is much subtler: the gradual contagion of nonjudgmental acceptance. The result of this contagion is that behavior that would have been roundly condemned forty years ago is now "understood" or in some cases even accepted.

Two college-student parents killed their newborn baby and left his body in a trash can outside a cheap motel. The pair received hundreds of calls of sympathy and support. After all, it was "understandable" that they panicked. In the end, a judge sentenced them to less than three years in prison.

In Wisconsin an expectant mother tried to poison her fetus with alcohol one day before the due date. She received no jail time, as supporters petitioned the press and the court with tales about her life of woe.

Throughout the country drug-addicted babies are routinely returned to the mothers who have already damaged them physically and perhaps limited their learning potential for life. But remember: The mother has a disease. Can society deprive the mother of raising her own children? Well, I damn well would. But I seem to be in the minority these days, as my "understanding" threshold does not reflect the society in which we live. In all the examples I've cited, the child's life is devalued in favor of the adult's "situation." How did this happen in America?

Here's my answer, which is the lead-in to our first encounter in the No Spin Zone: The welfare of a child means less today because of the promotion and acceptance of certain so-called special interests. The most notorious example—and I am not making this up—is an organization based in the United States called the North American Man-Boy Love Association. It advocates the legalization of sex between men and boys as young as *eight* years old. Read that sentence again and digest the eight-years-old part. This vile NAMBLA group was formed in 1978 and calls for the "empowerment" of youth in the sexual area. It says it does not engage in any activities that violate the law.

Oh yeah? What about the fact that NAMBLA was involved in funding an orphanage in Thailand that allowed grown men to rape and molest the children who lived there? And what about the case of child rape in Ohio where NAMBLA was found guilty of complicity in the crime? The Ohio Court of Appeals ruled that NAMBLA's literature, found in the possession of the rapist, showed "preparation and purpose" in encouraging the rape.

It gets much, much worse. A NAMBLA member recently

raped and murdered a young boy in Massachusetts. In October 1997 ten-year-old Jeffrey Curley was playing near his home in Cambridge when two men tried to lure him into a car. When he resisted, Salvatore Sicari and Charles Jaynes got brutal. They wound up killing the boy and then drove to Maine, where they dumped the boy's body in a river.

Both men were eventually arrested, convicted, and sentenced to life imprisonment. Prosecutors at the trial produced as critical evidence a diary kept by Jaynes. In it he flat out stated that he became obsessed with having sex with young boys *after* he joined NAMBLA. How did the organization allegedly poison him with its ideas? According to the diary, Jaynes received NAMBLA literature in the mail and visited the group's website on computers at the Boston Public Library. Clearly, these NAMBLA people wanted to get their message out. According to lawyers familiar with the website, it actually posted techniques designed to lure boys into having sex with men and also supplied information on what an adult should do if caught.

Jeffrey Curley's parents are suing NAMBLA in federal court for $200 million. And guess who is defending NAMBLA in the case? Can you spell ACLU? That's right. The most powerful free speech watchdog in the world is using its money and resources to make sure that NAMBLA is not driven out of business. Is this an outrage or what?

The amazing truth is that the American Civil Liberties Union is spending membership dues defending the lawsuit. In a statement it said, "Regardless of whether people agree with or abhor NAMBLA's views, holding the organization responsible for crimes committed by others who read their materials would gravely endanger our important First Amendment rights."

Baloney! I respect the ACLU's goal of protecting the rights of all Americans. At their best, this group is courageous in defending legitimate expressions of opinion, some of which, like the Nazi marches, are pretty vile. But NAMBLA is a different matter because the freedom to harm children is not built into our Constitution.

Attorney Floyd Abrams walked onto *The O'Reilly Factor* set confident and clear-eyed. He had won many of these debates in the past. In my introduction to the segment, I told the audience that I believed NAMBLA was guilty of promoting statutory rape and was a seditious organization in the sense that it wanted to undercut the moral foundation of the United States. Abrams opened his remarks by saying that "the ACLU serves the public by serving even an awful bunch of creeps." Then we got down to the heart of the matter and things got heated.

O'REILLY: This doesn't have anything to do with free speech.

ABRAMS: But of course it does.

O'REILLY: No, this has to do with aiding and abetting, promoting a crime on a website.

ABRAMS: If that's what they do, then the family will win the case. But until they show that, there should be somebody brave enough—and the ACLU is—to show up.

O'REILLY: I think you're dead wrong because what the ACLU is doing is allowing an organization to corrupt children. In doing so the ACLU becomes part of the crime if it wins and allows NAMBLA to get away with it.

ABRAMS: So they shouldn't have a lawyer, right?

O'REILLY: They shouldn't have the ACLU.

ABRAMS: Throw them in jail.

O'REILLY: I'd put them in jail in a heartbeat.

ABRAMS: I know *you* would.

O'REILLY: Each lawyer has a responsibility to choose the case that promotes justice.

ABRAMS: These people need the ACLU.

Sure they need it, because they are a criminal enterprise that exists for only one reason: to encourage statutory rape. The ACLU's representation is free, and NAMBLA is staying alive because of it. When the ACLU chooses which cases to take, it has a responsibility to the people who are paying dues to it. The thing is, no decent human being should be helping NAMBLA, and I know many ACLU members who are absolutely mortified that this organization has stained itself with this case.

It should be obvious that I am a big free speech supporter. The *Factor* would have been shut down a long time ago if the First Amendment wasn't sacred. But we need a clear-thinking ACLU to protect our freedom of expression, not some radical organization that is lost in a fog of self-righteousness. I asked ACLU President Nadine Strossen to address this NAMBLA issue, but she declined. That was interesting. Ms. Strossen has talked with me before and is anything but camera shy.

And what about the authorities? Why isn't the Justice Department prosecuting NAMBLA? If the Ohio court nailed them, what's wrong with the feds? The answer to that one is that the feds don't care. We have become a nation held hostage to self-serving rationalizations of special interest groups. The Zone is sickened by the cowardice of the Justice Department as well as by the ACLU's irresponsibility. Using the First Amendment as a cover for the subversion of our laws violates the public safety. Spinning the NAMBLA-ACLU deal as a "rights" issue is a disgrace.

"One thing [NAMBLA] didn't say was go out and kill anybody," Abrams said to me. "One thing it didn't say was go out and rape anybody."

But as any good citizen knows, it's not what you don't say that counts, it's what you do say. If the ACLU cannot acknowledge that it is a crime to conspire to have sex with children—a hurtful and brutal act physically, emotionally, and morally—then the American Civil Liberties Union does not deserve our respect or our support.

CHAPTER TWO

Reading, Writing, and

the Joy of Sex

ISSUE 2: Sex ed in your child's classroom
THE OPPONENT: Dr. Joycelyn Elders,
former surgeon general of the United States

O'REILLY: But you know how kids are. As soon as masturbation is brought up, they'll run out and tell their friends . . .
ELDERS: Poor children whom nobody has ever taught any-thing—are we to just throw them away? I think not.

It's not just the shameless perverts we need to worry about. Our children can also be assaulted by well-meaning public officials, teachers, and other adults in responsible positions. And these in-trusions on the young are far more powerful than the lurid crimes that grab headlines because they are often very personal and deliv-ered to the child one-on-one by influential adults.

Take the supposedly enlightened movement toward sex education. Right now, in many of the nation's public schools, there are sex education classes that get right to the heart of the matter. You get the what, you get the how. You get the birth control. You sometimes get nonverbal approval and, in rare cases, outright encouragement to engage in sexual activity. Driver's ed leads to driving a car, right? Sex ed has to be handled with the proper touch (pardon the pun) or, well, you get the idea.

I taught high school in Opa-locka, Florida, considered at the time to be one of the worst slums in South Florida. The kids at my school knew all about sex, drugs, and rock and roll. They needed guidance, not instruction. They needed emotional maturity and perspective. They listened very, very closely to everything an adult said about sex and especially the *way* it was said.

Sex ed for me was "the talk" my father gave me when I turned thirteen. It was awkward for both of us, as the Irish aren't exactly known for their Dr. Ruth–like candor in these matters. "The talk" was also somewhat unnecessary. I already knew the basics from seminars with my friends, using *Playboy* magazines as text. And my father's words were highly theoretical because the reality was, I had about as much chance of landing the great white whale as I did of having sex. Teenage girls want to date smooth guys. I was a barbarian. But I gave my father points for trying.

As a young teacher I was more relaxed speaking about sex than my father ever was, but I was careful. Students have a way of misquoting any provocative comments, and that can lead to big trouble in a Catholic high school. Some of my students as young as fifteen were having sex and almost everyone in the school knew about it. I encouraged the use of contraceptives for any American who did not want to become a parent. I spoke of this in a general sense, illuminating the lesson with specifics about poverty, divorce, and child deprivation. Most of the kids got the message. Some didn't. It is always that way.

Predictably, the school administration did not like my kind of direct approach. They were determined to control the sexuality of the students by threatening them with various punishments for risqué behavior. This of course was insane. The more you just say no, the more enticing certain kinds of behavior become. The issue came to a boil over football, of all things.

In Florida as in many parts of the country, Friday night high school football games are big. And because the weather in South Florida is hot until Thanksgiving, many of the high school girls were going to the games dressed like Anna Nicole Smith in full seduction mode. Hot pants and skimpy halter tops topped the dress hit parade. Many teachers were appalled.

A faculty meeting was called to discuss the menacing problem. One of the teachers asked what proper attire for football games actually was. Anyone? Anyone? Your humble correspondent rose to the occasion.

"Okay, proper attire for a football game," I said earnestly, "begins with shoulder pads, a helmet, knee and thigh pads, and spiked shoes, but *never* high heels."

A few of the male teachers actually laughed out loud but were silenced by the principal's stern glare. Most of the female teachers were aghast that I could be taking this desperate situation so lightly. But that's me—Bill Lite.

Anyway, the meeting was ridiculous and went on for hours. I headed for the men's room after about thirty minutes and never came back. The last thing I heard was somebody suggesting that navels be covered or something like that.

The next day I took my own kind of action. I told my coed

classes that young women who dress provocatively are usually seeking attention and would not be taken seriously by boys. How you dress, I suggested, shows the world what you think of yourself. So if a girl dresses like a tart or a boy like a bum, well . . .

Word got around campus fast. After that, only the hard-core kids continued to show up at games looking like *Baywatch* extras. They looked woefully out of place next to the students who got the message and dressed appropriately.

Teenagers can be persuaded to act responsibly if they are engaged in a relevant way. You don't have to set yourself up as the sex police; just talk sense. But right now in our nation's public schools, sense is on the run.

From 1993 to 1994 Dr. Joycelyn Elders was the surgeon general of the United States, a position that can be used to address the most stubbornly persistent of health-related social problems. I greatly admire her personally: She rose from an impoverished Arkansas childhood in a segregated black community to become a very successful pediatrician and then one of the most influential women in the country. Early in her career she served as a first lieutenant in the army. Later, then-governor Bill Clinton appointed her to head the Arkansas Department of Health.

An avowed and outspoken liberal, Dr. Elders got herself in trouble as surgeon general by saying that masturbation should be taught and promoted in the nation's public schools. In her view, such a practical alternative to intercourse would cut the rate of unwanted pregnancies and sexually transmitted diseases. After a crescendo of protest from the public and many officials, President Clinton fired her.

Dr. Elders is extremely permissive in other areas as well. She advocates the legalization of hard drugs as a way "to reduce the crime rate," and promotes abortion as a form of birth control. "I don't deal well with people who have a love affair with the fetus," she said memorably, "but won't take care of children." Her son was an intravenous drug user at one time, so she has a personal interest in America's narcotics problem.

A charming woman with an easy, engaging smile, she entered the No Spin Zone with enthusiasm. I happen to disagree with her, but I couldn't help liking her.

O'REILLY: You must have known you were going to get in trouble over the masturbation remarks.

ELDERS: Why?

O'REILLY: Come on. This is America!

ELDERS: Ninety percent of men and 70 percent of women masturbate, and the rest lie.

O'REILLY: Parents don't want it taught in school.

ELDERS: Nobody has to teach anybody. God taught us how to do it. But we should stop lying to children telling them hair will grow on their hands or they'll go blind or they'll go crazy.

O'REILLY: Why can't parents take care of that?

ELDERS: If all children had parents like you who would educate their children, talk about the drug issue, talk about teen pregnancy, talk about sexuality issues, we wouldn't have the problems.

O'REILLY: But, Doctor, surely you understand that some parents don't want a teacher, an outsider, talking to their children about such personal issues, and surely they have the right to demand that that not be done.

ELDERS: You're absolutely right. All they have to do is say that they don't want their children in that class.

O'REILLY: But you know how kids are. As soon as masturbation is brought up, they'll run out and tell their friends. So that really doesn't work.

ELDERS: Poor children whom nobody has ever taught anything—are we to just throw them away? I think not.

She's right on target that lack of information, of all kinds, hinders poor children in this country. But masturbation, in my opinion, was the wrong battlefield for making that point. Schools have no business teaching sexual technique of any kind, no matter what the well-meaning intention.

I can't believe that one parent in a thousand, or ten thousand, wants some teacher explaining how sex is *accomplished*. There are simply too many different attitudes about sex. If Dr. Elders were teaching the course at the local junior high, her acceptance of wholesale abortion would emerge. Another teacher might be equally permissive about homosexuality, or believe in total sexual abstinence before marriage, or think we'd all be better off physically and mentally if we practiced all the *Kama Sutra* positions. Talk about phys ed!

You get the picture. The individual's attitudes on this highly private, highly personal subject are always going to have an effect on the discussion. Not many of us would want our kids learning history from a dedicated communist or evolutionary science from someone who believes only in Adam and Eve. As a parent I don't want a teacher's sexual outlook passed along to my child.

But the repercussions of irresponsible sex? That's what *must* be taught. The links between irresponsible sex and poverty, divorce, violence, and disease should be drummed into every American kid from age ten onward. I mean pedal to the metal. And that's where Dr. Elders should concentrate her energies and persuasive skills. If she had, she would have accomplished so much more, not only for the poor children of this country but also for all the kids.

Here's the headline and the endgame regarding sex ed. Kids need a healthy dose of reality. Have a baby out of wedlock and there's a good chance you will be poor the rest of your life. Have unprotected sex—you could die. If you don't believe me, take a walk down any ghetto street. Visit any local hospice.

Sure, public schools can perform a valuable service by dispensing birth control—when a counselor agrees. You're never going to convince everybody to wait. But parents have rights too. And on the issue of sexual instruction, their rights have to be respected by Joycelyn Elders and everybody else. Government does not have the right to intrude into the fabric of the family. Learning sexual technique in high school is not going to get you into college and may get you on the welfare rolls. Give the kids and their parents a break, okay? Our schools should be G-rated institutions, at least in the classroom. Leave sex where it belongs—on television.

✳

While we're speaking of parenting, you might want to hear about Dr. Elders's own experience as the mother of a drug-abusing son. At one point she opined that more people die from using tobacco than from using illegal drugs, and she's right about that. Still, in my view, the corrupting influence of substance abuse has to be condemned by society. Just because we have problems with alcohol and tobacco doesn't mean we should add to those problems by legalizing more intoxicants.

I had to ask Dr. Elders if she was angry with the people who got her son involved with narcotics.

"No," she said frankly. "What I got really angry about was how we as a society and I as his mother didn't know enough to intervene effectively."

Dr. Elders took responsibility. She also took effective action. When we talked, her son had kicked his habit and was staying clean. Even though the doctor and I disagree on the solutions to these terrible problems, I know she is sincere in trying to help.

The goal of the Zone is not always to reach agreement, but to listen and consider—in other words, to think. And not to give in to, in Steve Allen's term, "dumbth." You'll see what I mean by that in the next chapter.

CHAPTER THREE

"Why? Because We Like You!"

ISSUE 3: Violence and sleaze in our living rooms

THE OPPONENT: Steve Allen, comedian and activist

ALLEN: The problem with TV, which comes into our homes, is that seven- and eight-year-old children are now seeing a hell of a lot of real vulgarity, and I haven't been able to hear anybody tell me that's good for the children or for the country.

O'REILLY: Do you think watching these programs makes kids want to have sex?

ALLEN: No. Mother Nature makes them want to have sex.

If you were a kid in the late 1950s, there's a good chance your thinking was shaped by two television programs, *The Mickey Mouse Club* and *Howdy Doody*. If you had asked me back then what I thought of these shows, I would have mocked them. Little wise guy that I was, I smirked at the sight of a bunch of kids wearing large rodent ears and grinning themselves into road maps of wrinkles. That, if you have to be told, was Mickey's gang, the Mouseketeers.

As for the hokey puppet show, I was annoyed enough to talk back to the black-and-white TV. "Hey, kids, what time is it?" some guy named Buffalo Bob yelled. A studio audience packed with kids screamed back, "*Howdy Doody* time!" This gave me such a headache, I can't tell you. And my reply to Buffalo Bob's time line was, "It's time for you to leave, buckskin man," or words to that effect. The whole thing enthralled my sister but put me in a foul mood. I can still hear Sis singing, "M-I-C—see you real soon—K-E-Y—why? Because we like you!" I was outraged! However, you will notice that more than forty years after first hearing these lines, *I still remember them*.

That's the power of the tube.

My little sister and most of the calmer kids in my Long Island neighborhood loved Howdy Doody and the Mouseketeers. They talked about them. They repeated the lame jokes. They wore rodent ears themselves. I couldn't figure it out. I also couldn't figure out why Mouseketeer Annette Funicello's sweatshirt kept expanding outward. It had a big picture of Mickey Mouse on it, and at the end of the second season of programs, the mouse on Annette's shirt looked like he had the mumps, if you know what I mean.

Anyway, if you could gather all the kids in the USA in one place today and you yelled, "Hey, kids, what time is it?" the answer would probably be "It's Stone Cold Steve Austin time." Or "*Melrose Place* time." Or perhaps "*Buffy the Vampire Slayer* time." Howdy and Buffalo Bob would be appalled.

The late Steve Allen was. In fact, he went so far as to blame the television industry for corrupting the nation's youth. Allen believed that programs dumbed kids down and encouraged antisocial behavior. He had the résumé to form that opinion. He invented *The Tonight Show* in the fifties and was a pioneer in TV comedy. Clean TV comedy.

Allen and the actress Shirley Jones (*The Partridge Family* mom) cochaired the Parents Television Council, which supported advertisements that asked the question "Are you fed up with steamy, unmarried sex situations, filthy jokes, perversion, vulgarity, violence, killings, etc.?" Bill Cosby and Tim Allen, among other celebrities, joined the PTC's crusade.

On a windy but warm day this legendary entertainer sat down across from me on our Los Angeles set. Steve Allen's toupee was slightly askew, but his eyes still danced with mischief and his familiar laugh was as hearty as ever. Here was a multitalented human being who seemed to want to make every moment enjoyable for himself and everyone around him. He seemed a bit tired but gave no evidence of the health problems that would kill him just a few months later. In the commercial break before his segment began, Allen was cheerful, but when the camera lights went on and the subject turned to the current state of American television, there was no mirth in his voice.

O'REILLY: Mr. Allen, you pose the question "Are you fed up with steamy, unmarried sex situations, filthy jokes, perversion, vulgarity, violence, killings, etc.?" Wow, you're not mincing any words here!

ALLEN: No, my word-mincer broke. The main thing is, all of that is legit. It's all documented.

O'REILLY: When I was a kid, I watched *The Untouchables* and *Combat*. It didn't make me violent.

ALLEN: There's a difference between the problem of sexual vulgarity and violence. You are never going to be able to totally get rid of violence. First of all, it's a part of the world and you can't do a show about World War II or the Mafia and not have blood and guns and foul language, because that's part of reality, and I don't object to that. I don't want six-year-old people to see it, but I don't object to it. But the problem with television, which comes into our homes, is that seven- and eight-year-old children are now seeing a hell of a lot of real vulgarity, and I haven't been able to hear anybody tell me that's good for the children or for the country.

O'REILLY: Do you think that watching these programs will make kids want to have sex?

ALLEN: No. Mother Nature makes them want to have sex. The argument is that when sexual material is dealt with on television and nobody has to worry about birth control or sexual disease, then the implication is, "Hey, it's all kind of cute and hip and let's do it even though I've never met you before."

O'REILLY: So you believe kids are impressionable enough to pick up a message like "They're having fun at Beverly Hills High. I should have fun at my school"?

ALLEN: Yeah, I believe that. There's a lot of documentation. This is not just some theory of mine. I am by no means a saint. But the sleaze and vulgarity on TV disgust even an old roué like me. It's part of the whole dumbing down, the coarsening. The question is, what kinds of parents are the kids today going to make? I think the answer is, not too good.

O'REILLY: Why?

ALLEN: Well, imagine an ideal father. Would you like it if he came home with a couple of broads on each arm? You see that image on TV.

O'REILLY: Are you referring to President Clinton?

ALLEN: That's another matter. But really, if people don't know we have a problem here, then we are in worse shape than I thought.

Steve Allen was right, of course. Society has become coarser because of lazy parents and an exploitative entertainment industry. The stuff that kids are exposed to on TV and in the movies and listening to on CDs has an enormous influence on them. If they don't have strong counterinfluences, watch out. And it's not only fictional television in play. Some of the most influential people in our society—like Bill Clinton, Jesse Jackson, Robert Downey, Jr., and Darryl Strawberry, just to name a few—provide dismal examples to the nation's youth. TV news lasers in on these guys and brings their lurid stories home—to your home. Where little Melissa and Scott are taking it all in.

But Steve Allen was fighting a losing battle. This country hates censorship and loves money. Sleazy entertainment aimed at kids makes a lot of money. And the only way to stop it is for the government to censor it. That is not going to happen and the entertainment industry is not going to police itself. Everybody in Hollywood has to make money in order to work. And few of these people are creative enough to do that without wallowing in the mud. Their jobs are more important than your kids—at least to them. And they are calling the shots in the wonderful world of entertainment.

Parents, that's your cue again. The TV set is an inanimate object that requires electricity and perhaps cable fees in order to beam stuff into your house. Meaning: You control it, not the other way around. No parent has to wait for the V chip or another kind of high-tech blockade. Just monitor what your kids see.

And when something objectionable gets through your safety net, a smart parent can actually turn a disgusting piece of television into a life lesson. Engage your child in conversation about a questionable activity. Sex in sitcoms, misleading advertising, vulgar language can all be made into interesting discussions (note the word "discussions," and go easy on the lectures). Your kids need to learn how TV entertainment and advertising work so they will not be prone to accepting mindless propaganda.

Of course, irresponsible and lazy parents will not provide a buffer between the media madness and their kids. Those kids will suffer. That is life in a free society.

At another point in our conversation, Steve Allen made a related point: "The question is, what kind of husbands and wives will our kids make? . . . If they are buying into the coarse television at an early age, what kind of adults will they become?"

✳

Can we bring back Howdy Doody? Sure, about the time Calvin Coolidge becomes a household name again. And as I said, I would have rather mowed the lawn than watched Howdy. Even so, something about that darned puppet made me think he was a real person. Buffalo Bob told me that everybody thought Howdy was real. A slight exaggeration but one with heart.

How did Bob make that happen? Maybe it was because he wanted to help kids rather than exploit them for cash, and the kids could sense that. Buffalo Bob was a no spin kind of guy. I did the last interview with him before he died at his home in Hendersonville, North Carolina, on July 30, 1998. He was eighty and sharp as a blade.

O'REILLY: My father used to come home from work looking like a rumpled version of Robert Young in *Father Knows Best*. You know, a suit, white shirt, and thin tie. So I'd go, "Hey, Dad, why don't you dress like Buffalo Bob?" And he'd give me that look.

BUFFALO BOB: I used that look too and it worked wonders. Believe me.

O'REILLY: Yeah, but you didn't need a look. No kid wanted to be yelled at by Buffalo Bob. Even I didn't want that. Do you see any difference between the children of the 1950s and today?

BUFFALO BOB: I really don't think there's an awful lot of difference and I'll tell you why. I think kids are kids. All kids like slapstick, all kids like fantasy. Kids laugh at the same things today that Clarabell and I did fifty years ago.

O'REILLY: So even though children have computers and ninety channels of television, they're still laughing at the same dopey stuff?

BUFFALO BOB: There's no doubt about it. Kids know right away whether or not they like you. One time I got sick and this guy from NBC was called in to replace me. He bombed. After the show he said to me, "When I walked in and saw those forty little monsters there at the peanut gallery defying me to make them laugh, I knew I was dead. They knew right away that I couldn't stand them."

O'REILLY: So that was the secret to your success. You actually liked the kids.

BUFFALO BOB: It was as simple as that.

He was right. Little kids laugh at the same stuff they always laughed at, and they instinctively know who the bad guys are. But in today's media-swamped society, that instinct goes south with age, and today children grow up too fast. By age eight or nine they're used to seeing and hearing things that would have been out of place in an army barracks thirty years ago. Do you even know about these things? Do you ever listen to the lyrics blasting upstairs or on the car radio? Or are you just grateful when they use earphones and seem to be boppin' happily in the backseat?

If you don't already know about the messages Puff Daddy and Eminem shout out from their pedestals atop the rap world, well, listen up.

CHAPTER FOUR

The Sound of

Four-Letter Music

ISSUE 4: Sex and violence in your kid's headphones

THE OPPONENT: Sean "Puff Daddy" Combs, rap star

COMBS: . . . We had to sing our problems away and we had to sing to help get things better. And right now that's the way a rap song may feel to an inner-city kid who has to deal with being trapped in a bad situation.

O'REILLY: But do you go too far with the cop-killing lyrics and the bitch stuff?

Even if you wouldn't be caught dead listening to rap music, it is hard to avoid this guy Puff Daddy. He is in the newspaper nearly every week. Dating Jennifer Lopez, being charged with crimes, being sued by the mother of his son. The Puff Meister is one big man-about-town.

At age thirty-two Sean Combs is a multimillionaire rap singer and producer who parties with people like Donald Trump and Martha Stewart. He swaggers around Manhattan with a "posse" of hangers-on, drinking champagne in nightclubs and holding court in expensive restaurants. Of course by exposing himself to the late-night rap world, Combs has brought a heap of trouble onto himself. Here's a partial résumé:

In 1996 Combs was convicted of criminal mischief for threatening a photographer in New York City. In 1999 he was charged with ordering the beating of record executive Steve Stoute. In that fracas Stoute's jaw and arm were broken. Combs pleaded guilty and a judge sentenced him to *one day* in an anger management course. Perhaps Combs should have ordered the judge beaten after that kind of foolish sentence.

Just a few months later, Combs was back in court, this time charged with gun possession and bribery in connection with the nightclub shootings of two bystanders. After a trial where one of the shooting victims flat out identified Combs as pointing a pistol at her, he was acquitted. But then you probably knew that.

I call the guy "Puff the Magic Raggin" and feel it is a shame that his decadent lifestyle is being played out in front of millions of his young fans. And I believe it is safe to say that a good portion of those fans do not have an emotional support system in place which can put Combs's irresponsible actions into perspective. The babes, the bucks, the busts, and the acquittals look kind of glamorous from behind deprived eyes. Self-indulgence is the message received. Discipline, the most important ingredient in achieving lasting success, is not a part of the Puff Daddy world.

Now, there's nothing strange about kids going nuts over new music and young performers who drive parents up the wall. Frank Sinatra became an establishment legend, but the frenzy of his female fans in his early days made many parents nervous. I was just a little kid when Elvis Presley gyrated his hips into the national spotlight. Just the week before, it seemed, the "big kids" in the neighborhood all looked like members of the Kingston Trio, complete with flattop haircuts. Then, suddenly, Vinnie and Eddie and Jimmy had greasy pompadours and sneers on their upper lips.

So don't tell me a pop star isn't a huge influence on kids. I mean, to this day there are adult Americans who think of Elvis daily. Who still idolize him. And a few in Vegas who *have turned into* him.

When the Beatles arrived from England in the early sixties, pop culture turned into the dominant moneymaking entertainment vehicle in the country. Some parents became very concerned when their kids adopted cockney accents, but my father had just two words: "great gimmick."

This time the neighborhood was awash in bowl haircuts. A few guys even began calling each other "bloke." Many of my friends got together and formed bands. I am proud to say that even early on I was a contrarian, and Beatlemania did not affect me. I was a Beach Boys kind of guy.

But it was not until the late sixties that the influence of rock people really kicked in with a behavior-altering intensity. Everybody under the age of thirty in the Age of Aquarius knew that people like Jimi Hendrix, Janis Joplin, and Jim Morrison were heavily into intoxicants. None of them lived beyond that dreaded age of thirty, but all had tremendous influence.

Drugs and rock went together like Ozzie and Harriet. Songs celebrating drug use dominated the charts. In my neighborhood at least six of my friends became heavily addicted. When the Jefferson Airplane sang about "feeding your head," it sounded seductive. Why not groove along to their music and get wasted when it looked like so much fun? Well, it wasn't long before the fun ended in two funerals. Two of my guys lost their lives because of drug abuse. At least five others lost their innocence and were never the same even after rehab. The "groove" they found didn't pay off in gold records; it paid off in continuing guilt and inner pain.

Fast-forward to the present . . . Some kids out there are watching every move Puffy Combs makes, and this should be troubling to anyone who cares about the question Steve Allen posed: What kind of adults will these kids be? Sample what Puff Daddy feeds them on one of his smash-mouth CDs:

> I'm a Goodfella kinda lady,
> Stash 380's and Mercedes, Puffy hold me down baby!
> Only female in my crew, and I kick s—— like a nigga do,
> with a trigga too, f—— you.

In case you're wondering, that's what passes for creativity in the world of Sean Combs and is typical of the stuff he puts out. With those lyrics and further dollar signs on his mind, Sean "Puff Daddy" Combs visited the No Spin Zone to promote an album. To many in show business, this was scarcely believable. Puff Daddy and O'Reilly? But he showed up, all 5'7" of him strutting into the studio. He was decked out in a white T-shirt, khaki short pants, and sneakers. Followed by an entourage of ten, he checked the lights, the set, the crew. Obviously, he was used to being in control.

Finally, he was ready to go and he sat across from your humble correspondent with a look of bored detachment. He didn't stay bored for long.

O'REILLY: People are under the impression that rap music and this rap world is a violent gangster-ridden corrupt enterprise.

COMBS: That's definitely a wrong impression. We live in a world where you definitely have bad apples at times, but bad apples can't spoil the whole bunch. That's not a fair label to put on rap. There's problems but there's problems in all parts of the world. Hip-hop and rap is part of the world.

O'REILLY: There is a synergy between you and some giant companies, the establishment corporations that put out your product. Here you guys are renegades, talking about the street and the inner city, and the guys in the suits are making bundles of dough off you guys.

COMBS: I have a joint venture situation. And also I'm sitting there with them with a suit on, and I'm telling them what I want. They don't tell me what to do. It's a partnership.

O'REILLY: You're making them a lot of money.

COMBS: Excuse me. They don't look at me like I'm a renegade rapper or anything like that. They look at me as a businessman. I'm somebody that has intelligence, that went to college. They look at me as the same human being you are. I mean you may be looking at me as a renegade rapper, but I'm looking at you as a human being. We don't look at each other the same.

O'REILLY: Is rap good for the young people of America?

COMBS: Rap music is our modern-day Negro spiritual like it's a music that was first started and was prominent in the cities for young black America. And it's like when I say old Negro spiritual, when we came over here and we were in bondage, we were slaves and we were in the cotton fields. We had to sing our problems away, and we had to sing to help things get better. And right now that's the way a rap song may feel to an inner-city kid who has to deal with being trapped in a bad situation.

O'REILLY: But do you go too far with the cop-killing lyrics and the bitch stuff?

COMBS: Anything in life can be taken too far. You know sometimes the news is taken too far. Music is no different. Everybody has to be accountable or responsible for their own actions and that's what I try to do. The rap world is not bad. It's not a negative situation. The rap world has created a lot of jobs for inner-city youths. It's been an outlet and a source of power—economic power for us to start and do our things.

Negro spirituals were songs of longing for freedom; in an odd, circuitous way, I grant Combs his point that inner-city lyrics can speak to the problems of poor children in a society that might seem to have no place for them. But does a thirteen-year-old really get that sociopolitical message from a rapper who rants about whores and guns and bitches and booze?

The stark truth about the inner city is that the children born there have the odds stacked against them from day one of their lives. You don't have to be a bleeding-heart liberal to see that. Remember when Richard Nixon said that if he had been born black he would have been a Black Panther? He may have been exaggerating to gain sympathy, but all clear-thinking Americans know that the factors necessary for a young person to gain maturity are often unavailable to inner-city kids.

For anyone, the road to success in America is full of potholes and challenges. In order to succeed and prosper, all children need love and discipline. They don't need to become a "Goodfella kinda lady . . . with a trigga."

Puff Daddy, as he argues, may be welcomed in the boardrooms of the big entertainment corporations—as long as he holds on to his avid following. But other young people with no command of the English language and chips on their tattooed shoulders have little chance.

Combs could lead by example; his lyrics could speak to the drive that has made him successful. Instead, he paints a gross picture completely lacking in perspective. Somewhere over the Jordan, perhaps, a great spiritual singer of the past like Harry T. Burleigh or Roland Hayes is weeping. "Little lambs, I hear you calling," sang Hayes, evoking the pain of enslaved people. Combs, in my opinion, is rapping out a message that if followed will continue that enslavement.

※

If you are not disgusted by now, hold on. There is something far more insidious on the rap scene than Sean Combs, who may even be over the hill. Grammy Award winner Eminem is a nasty piece of work whose recordings have sold in the tens of millions.

Born Marshall Mathers in Warren, Michigan, twenty-nine years ago, Eminem fills his recordings with vivid images of drug use, rape, mother abuse, and even murder. But rock reviewers rave about his "genius." He calls homosexuals "faggots," yet gay icon Elton John fawns over him, and the two do a duet on the Grammy telecast. Screwed-up John explained that he wanted to "celebrate" Eminem's artistry. Swell. For me it was just two creepy guys onstage for five minutes.

The bible of rock music, *Rolling Stone* magazine, says that Eminem is a champion of the "white underclass." Rubbish. Like the black rappers he imitates, the guy is exploiting angry kids who listen to him. If they're disenfranchised, he encourages their rage, not their liberation. Will he let loose his millions to pay bail when someone acts out the violence and antisocial acts he encourages? Will he pay the rent of fans who don't have the social skills to hold a decent job? Will he fund shelters for battered women?

Doubt it.

By the way, you might be interested to know that the tattoo ol'

Eminem sports on his skinny arm celebrates the drug Vicodin, a narcotic that is currently the rage in Hollywood. "Hey, Eminem is totally stoked on Vicodin, man, let's try some." Don't think kids don't think that—and act on it.

But, like, come on, man. You are missing what Eminem is saying. Take a look at the "artistry."

> Girl and Boy groups, all you do is annoy me.
> So I have been sent here to destroy you.
> And there's a million of us, just like me
> Who just don't give a f——like me.

That's the cleanest excerpt I could find that made any sense.

Because Marshall Mathers uses four-letter words every two seconds, you can't interview him on a news program, even though I would dearly love to do so. But Alan Light, the editor in chief of *Spin* magazine, did enter the Zone to stick up for Mathers. *Spin* magazine (no relation to the No Spin Zone) is a huge factor in the marketing of pop music and is known for jumping on the latest pop fads. Eminem has been on the cover of *Spin* a number of times. His mom would have been very proud except for the fact that part of Eminem's act is to debase his mom and even threaten to beat her to a pulp. Be that as it may, *Spin* hit No Spin and here's how it played out.

ALAN LIGHT: I like Eminem. I don't like everything that he says. I think some of it's repellent. But I think he's clearly talented.

O'REILLY: In what way talented?

LIGHT: He can rhyme words. He can tell stories. He can write fiction.

O'REILLY: All right. I know I'm an old fogy so you've got to tell me this. Anybody can rhyme words. I can do that all day long. What stories is he telling that are worth hearing?

LIGHT: Well, they are often ugly stories or violent stories, but so are the stories of Stephen King or Martin Scorsese or any number of artists. He has an audience that understands when he is writing fiction, when he is writing for shock value.

O'REILLY: I hear his demographic is twenty-three and younger.

LIGHT: That's probably safe. He's a pop star to teenagers.

O'REILLY: Here's my problem. He's appealing to people ages twelve to twenty-three and he's telling them I hate my mother, I hate my wife—she's a "ho." He's telling them he hates gays and he's thinking about killing people.

LIGHT: He says things that are objectionable, there's no question. But there is a genre, there is an audience that understands the language he is speaking.

O'REILLY: But why is the entertainment industry lionizing him if he's picking on minority groups and putting them in a hateful category?

LIGHT: Because there is talent there. There is a visceral thrill that people get from things that are deliberately there to shock.

O'REILLY: I'm not going to discuss talent, because talent is in the eye of the beholder. But I will tell you that throughout history some of the worst people on earth have been talented people, and I don't think that just because you're talented you should be applauded.

LIGHT: He's not being rewarded for being a good person. He's being rewarded for his artistry and for the writing on the records he makes. Millions of people have bought them, and the question is not what he is saying; the question is why it is touching such a chord.

O'REILLY: Well, let me just tell you, Mr. Light. *Mein Kampf* also sold millions of copies. Thanks for being here.

The Eminem thing somewhat parallels the NAMBLA situation that we talked about in chapter one. Forty years ago Eminem could not have existed as an entertainer in America. His rhymes about terrorizing homosexuals at knifepoint and brutally raping women would have been rejected in the entertainment marketplace and he himself would have been an outcast.

But I'm not for censoring him (because, as I've said, I don't want anyone censoring me). However, I can condemn Eminem and encourage others to do the same. Don't let your kids buy his records. Period.

As we'll see in upcoming chapters, Jesse Jackson and Al Sharpton call for boycotts when they find a business they believe is being harmful to blacks. Why can't good people of all colors call for a boycott of Eminem and other hateful rap "artists"? It wouldn't completely work, of course, but it would get the attention of the record company and perhaps embarrass some of these corporate vampires. But don't count on any help from the Reverends Jackson and Sharpton. They don't take stands that might be unpopular with their base.

Right now the last thing the record companies are worried about is a national rebellion on the part of concerned parents. Where are the concerned parents anyway? Seven million kids bought Eminem's last CD. Do the parents think it isn't that bad?

It is.

Eminem's success has taught everybody that a hater can acquire wealth and fame. Nice lesson. The Stones sang about it in the classic song, "Sympathy for the Devil." Eminem can play the lead in the movie.

The last word on this is that Elvis has indeed left the building and taken all shreds of decency with him. Eminem is subversive, destructive, and damaging to the ignorant minds that take him seriously. We have given him a safe harbor in America to spread his poisonous audio graffiti. That is the price of a free society. The true no spin on this is that *we* should be much more angry with Eminem than he is with us.

CHAPTER FIVE

The Laura Antidote

ISSUE 5: Tough talk on moms, kids, and work

THE OPPONENT: Dr. Laura Schlessinger

O'REILLY: So you believe you can't be a good parent and work at the same time?

DR. LAURA: Children are helpless, defenseless, dependent little entities that require us to be there. There is no paid help that will have the commitment and investment in your child in terms of religion and warmth and bonding and caring.

You surely know about Dr. Laura. She is as far away from the rap music scene as one could get. Yet she is a rapper herself, a relationship rapper. Call her radio show with your problems, and she's likely to send you to the woodshed. She wants people to do the right thing. Stop whining and seize control.

And Dr. Laura has something else in common with Eminem:

They're both on the outs with America's gay community. But there's a huge difference. While the thuggish rapper threatens to assault gays physically, the moralistic Dr. Laura argues that homosexuality is sinful. Strangely, the gay lobby sees this as more of a threat than the knife Eminem raps about. Homosexual activists urged sponsors to boycott Dr. Laura's TV program and some did. They have made her life miserable. Yes, the gay lobby protested Eminem but not nearly with the same intensity as they used in the Laura situation.

Dr. Laura Schlessinger is an interesting woman. She is extremely judgmental and her conservative approach to life and child rearing angers those who don't see things her way. Instead of simply disagreeing, they attack her in very personal ways. The reason is that unlike the moronic Eminem, who can be easily dismissed as a troglodytic fad by those who dislike him, Dr. Laura has captured the attention of Middle America by advocating a return to a traditional society, one that some believe is prejudicial and narrowminded. In her world Eminem and his ilk are social outcasts and any kind of so-called deviant behavior is confronted. The gay stuff gets the headlines, but it is Laura's child-raising theories that really drive some Americans crazy.

The National Organization for Women is absolutely furious at Dr. Laura for expressing her views, even though NOW's leadership have their mouths wide open on dozens of social issues. Her book *Parenthood by Proxy: Don't Have Them If You Won't Raise Them* was not exactly popular among NOW members. But it made the best-seller lists nonetheless.

When you get so many people so angry, you might be doing something right, or you might be a loon. To find out which, I invited Dr. Laura to the No Spin Zone. A small, intense woman, she is surrounded by an apprehensive staff who are very protective of her. She is genuinely angry at the decline of American morals—yet has had her own escapades in the past, including some embarrassing nude photos and a rift in her own family that at the time I interviewed her was still unresolved.

But none of us lead perfect lives, and I believe Dr. Laura is sincere and brave enough to state her case and take the heat—especially about child rearing.

O'REILLY: When I was growing up, my parents believed in "spare the rod, spoil the child." It was a punitive household and there was immediate punishment for any misbehavior. Most of the kids in my neighborhood were raised the same way. My theory is that many baby boomers are now overcompensating with their own kids and being too lenient. What do you think?

DR. LAURA: I'm not sure that's the reason. I think there's so much emphasis on personal gratification and fulfillment and entitlement in this country, we are so busy doing other things, that by the time we come home from work we don't want to have the stress and strain of holding children accountable for their actions. We don't want to discipline them and teach them. I also feel with the chaos of divorce, shacking up, remarriages, making more kids, love affairs, all of this nonsense going on, that parents feel a lot of guilt. So there is tiredness at the end of the day and guilt at the end of the day. The result is undisciplined children.

O'REILLY: So you believe you can't be a good parent and work at the same time?

DR. LAURA: Children are helpless, defenseless, dependent little entities that require us to be there. There is no paid help that will have the commitment and investment in your child in terms of religion and warmth and bonding and caring. Nobody's going to love the child like Mommy and Daddy.

O'REILLY: Isn't there a middle ground here where you can hire a nanny for a few hours a day?

DR. LAURA: There is no middle ground for the kids. I am saying there are shoulds and people are doing some things wrong and it's hurting the children. A lot of these people go on the defensive. It interferes with their permissiveness and their freedom to do whatever they want.

O'REILLY: You're right. Many people are taking your words very personally and they don't like you.

DR. LAURA: I am in the workplace but our family has always worked around our son. I work when he's in school. There are millions of hardworking families who manage their schedules so they are there for their kids.

O'REILLY: Yeah, but some people have intense schedules; they have no choice.

DR. LAURA: Intense schedules are a choice.

O'REILLY: Come on, Doctor, I need my female producers here for eight hours. They can't be home and carry this job.

DR. LAURA: Fine. Then they either need a man at home or not have the kids until they're in a different place in their careers.

O'REILLY: I disagree with you. That is too tough. I think a responsible caregiver can supervise the child for a few hours a day without harm.

DR. LAURA: You're starting to really crunch me.

O'REILLY: No, I just disagree with you on this one.

Look at today's reality in America. Families have to deal with a tough dance card. The cost of housing and modern conveniences is significant, and taxes are gutting the take-home pay of the working class. By necessity, most Americans have to work longer and harder than they might like. If you have more than two children, chances are both parents will have to work at least part-time.

Of course Dr. Laura is correct on the essentials: Children need a calm environment, focused affection, consistency, and discipline. Working parents can provide those necessities if they are willing to engage and stimulate the child when they are at home. Day care is risky, no doubt about it. Exposure at a young age to undisciplined or troubled children at a center can cause angst in your own child. The bacteria count in some of these places is off the chart and the supervision is out of your hands. The gently smiling caregiver might be a simpleton who sets the kids down in front of a TV and does little else. Not a great situation any way you slice it unless you get lucky. There are excellent day-care facilities but if your kid is in one, make sure you drop in unannounced from time to time.

A trusted nanny or baby-sitter is far more expensive but can help children immensely, and here is where I disagree with the absolutist approach taken by Dr. Laura. Children can bond with a variety of adults, as extended families have proved throughout the ages. As long as the adult genuinely cares for the child, there is no harm so long as the parents remain the centerpiece of the child's life, and that can be done by making yourself a dramatic presence, an authority figure the child loves and with whom he or she feels safe.

Neither Dr. Laura nor anyone else has the right to make working mothers feel guilty. American women have pursued careers and raised fine families at the same time. However, these dual purposes must be carefully thought out and executed with precision. Children should always get first priority, and if trouble develops, the job has to be put aside.

Needless to say, stay-at-home mothers should be admired, because this is a noble endeavor. But I also know plenty of stay-at-home moms who are neurotic messes, and I know a lot of working mothers who are far more effective caregivers to their children. Like most everything else in life, child raising is not a black or white deal.

Whatever the situation, the most important factor is the force of personality a parent brings to the home. That trumps any outside influence on a child. Call me controlling if you want, but I can guarantee you that the artistry of Eminem will not be heard in my house. And I do not feel guilty about employing a baby-sitter. I control my environment and make sure my child is secure and loved. That's all any parent can do. Life is tough and people have to work in order to provide security for their children. Dr. Laura is right to encourage the close parental supervision of children, but she errs in believing it can only be done one way. The kids know if you truly care for them or not. And they know if you're selfish and distant from them emotionally. Take all the time you can to be with your children, and home in on their needs. Do this and the impression you'll make will override their anxiety when you're gone. Affection and consistency will rule the day.

And one more thing: Lose the guilt about being overly "strict." Your kid is your responsibility, and if you think that Eminem and Puff Daddy and violent video games and professional wrestling and promiscuous TV programs do not reflect your view of life, then impose a No Fly Zone on this kind of entertainment. Hey, Junior, this kind of garbage just "doesn't fly" in this house. The No Fly Zone is first cousin to the No Spin Zone and like No Spin requires a well-thought-out explanation so the young ones don't think you have entered your Napoleon phase. But once the explanation is given, the No Fly Zone should be rigorously enforced and all the whining in the world shouldn't change that.

Finally, I do agree with Dr. Laura's book subtitle: "Don't Have Them If You Won't Raise Them." Little kids aren't golf bags you can store in the attic when you get sick of them. They are there for eighteen lonnnnng years. If you're Irish or Italian, maybe longer. On that Dr. Laura and I agree, and I appreciated it when she said to me, "It's people like you who agree half the time and not half the time, but at least are willing to listen to the ideas."

Fair enough, Doctor. That's what the No Spin Zone is all about.

CHAPTER SIX

Suddenly Susan

ISSUE 6: Sticking it to the cops

THE OPPONENT: Susan Sarandon, actress and activist

SARANDON: If you were a black person living in the city, you would experience the police in a completely different way.

O'REILLY: Well, maybe I would. But if I were a black person living in the city, I would know that the murder rate has fallen from 1,946 to 667, and most of those murders were in my neighborhood. I'd be pretty damned appreciative of that.

SARANDON: This is what a white person says when he's talking about civil liberties being taken away from someone who's not you.

Outspoken and feisty, Susan Sarandon would seem to be a natural for the No Spin Zone. For decades she has championed a smorgasbord of liberal causes while turning in superb film performances. Many men reading this right now will flash back to the lemon scene in the movie *Atlantic City*. Her role as Janet in *The Rocky Horror Picture Show* put her on the map, and in 1996 she won the Best Actress Oscar playing a nun in *Dead Man Walking*. This was not that great a stretch, since she graduated from Catholic University in 1969 under her maiden name, Susan Abigail Tomalin.

For years I had been trying to convince Ms. Sarandon to enter the No Spin Zone. She turned me down over and over. I am Lucifer to the crowd she runs with because I don't feel guilty about societal ills. Hell, I'm *trying* to improve things. Ms. Sarandon made plenty of enemies with her opposition to the Gulf War and her strident stance against the use of force by the police. She is the poster girl for what they now call "progressive" thought. I'm not exactly sure what that is, but I do know that Rush Limbaugh frowns upon it and the *Nation* magazine plumps for it.

To my surprise Susan suddenly changed her mind and entered hell—uh, the No Spin Zone. Why? Well, she was hot about the Amadou Diallo killing. Mr. Diallo, you may remember, was the African immigrant who was gunned down by four policemen in a Bronx neighborhood in New York City. Mr. Diallo was unarmed and had done nothing wrong. There was no reason for killing him.

A couple of days after the killing, Susan Sarandon, Al Sharpton, and the usual suspects began demonstrating against police brutality in New York. I felt that the displays of anger were justified but not the condemnation of the entire police force of some forty thousand officers.

In fact, the Internal Affairs Division was actively investigating the Diallo tragedy, and subsequently indictments were brought against the four officers, all members of a Street Crimes Unit. These units were controversial because their mandate was to remove guns from the street. These plainclothes officers would often "pat down" people they suspected of carrying guns, and Ms. Sarandon and others considered this a violation of a person's constitutional rights. Despite the controversy, the technique was effective: Tens of thousands of guns were confiscated and violent crime fell significantly in the areas where Street Crimes Units were operating.

After a lengthy trial, all four officers involved in the Diallo shooting were acquitted by a mixed-race jury. The jury believed the defense's claim that when one officer accidentally tripped while approaching Mr. Diallo, the other officers thought he was shot and began firing. That's what the jury believed; I wasn't there, so what do I know?

But Sarandon and her crew, also not present, were having none of that acquittal stuff. Energized by her convictions, she entered the No Spin Zone and sat across from me ready to do rhetorical battle. She is a true believer.

O'REILLY: By most accounts, aggressive police work in New York City has led to a remarkable drop in violent crime. You have thousands of people alive today because of aggressive policing. So why are you demonizing the police?

SARANDON: Well, first of all, that's a leading question because what happened was that there was an incident during which forty-four shots were fired and there was no indictment. Now, the way this country works is when something goes wrong you're supposed to examine it. So what I got arrested for was asking for some kind of action. I wasn't demonizing the police. If you don't ask that certain people be held responsible, you're inferring that all the police can do this kind of thing and get away with it. And the Street Crimes Unit was out of control.

O'REILLY: The mistake I think you're making is that there was an ongoing investigation and the system had to wait for the evidence to be presented to the grand jury. That's how the justice system works.

SARANDON: You have to admit there have been some things that have gone wrong.

O'REILLY: Sure, I do. And in any police force the size of New York's with forty thousand officers you're going to have a certain percentage that are bad.

SARANDON: And you think it takes months to get that kind of investigation when a white person is killed? I don't think that's true.

O'REILLY: I don't look at things in black and white terms.

SARANDON: Well, you don't have to, because you're white. If you were a black person living in the city, you would experience the police in a completely different way.

O'REILLY: Well, maybe I would. But if I were a black person living in the city, I would know that the murder rate has fallen from 1,946 to 667, and most of those murders were in my neighborhood. I'd be pretty damned appreciative of that.

SARANDON: This is what a white person says when he's talking about civil liberties being taken away from someone who's not you. I mean, it depends on what price you pay to have your neighborhood safe. And when you have everybody being picked up because of the color of their skin, it's not right.

O'REILLY: I would have been marching with you and I would have been on your side if the grand jury had not issued indictments. But you guys jumped the gun, demonized the police, and turned it into a racial issue. Do you think those four cops wanted to go out that night and kill a black guy? Is that what you think?

SARANDON: I think that those guys were so stressed by a quota system to try to bring people in that they were set up in a way which was not fair to them as well as not fair to Mr. Diallo.

O'REILLY: Certainly there was stress involved. There always is in high-crime neighborhoods. But the NYPD has been very effective in fighting crime and their duty is to protect us.

SARANDON: At what cost?

O'REILLY: I don't see the cost you see. I don't see black neighborhoods terrorized.

SARANDON: Well, you should go to a black neighborhood.

O'REILLY: I have many, many times. Ms. Sarandon, we respect your opinion, thanks for coming in.

After that lively discussion Ms. Sarandon almost ripped her blouse trying to get her microphone off. She left in a huff asking one of my producers, "What's his problem?" Susan, I don't know where to begin. But thanks for coming into the Zone.

Even though she thinks I'm a philistine, I like Ms. Sarandon. She does an enormous amount of unheralded charity work and is not a Hollywood phony. She truly believes that our system of justice tends to be racist, and to some extent she's right.

But having covered hundreds of ghetto stories and reported on police departments all across America, I can tell you that the vast majority of law enforcement people would put their lives on the line in a heartbeat to protect a person in danger, no matter what his or her color. Ms. Sarandon reacts emotionally to tragic incidents like the Amadou Diallo case, and the demagogues who profit from racial division use that emotion to further their own destructive agenda. A big Hollywood star like Susan Sarandon or Martin Sheen or any of the other social crusaders guarantees big media coverage.

What Ms. Sarandon does not get is the big picture. Violent

crime and drug dealing in the nation's minority precincts are often completely out of control. The police who patrol these areas are sometimes frightened and always on the defensive. They are tense, and this often leads to aggression and poor judgment. We are talking about human nature here, not institutional racism. Yes, there is racial profiling and yes, it is wrong. But racial profiling brings a higher arrest count. Does the end justify the means? No, it does not. But the intent, for the most part, is not to terrorize black people—the intent is to protect them from criminal predators who threaten them every day.

Why isn't Susan Sarandon demonstrating against drug dealing and the activities of violent felons? Surely, these things are just as bad as unwarranted police stops. Surely, these things hurt minorities and the poor. Hey, I'll make her a sign if she'll march with me.

Members of the left in America are often well intentioned, but they are just as often clueless. There will always be corrupt and racist cops because there will always be corrupt and racist people. But police officers on the street get up every day knowing that they might not come home that night. And for this they should be given the benefit of any doubt. The police should be closely scrutinized because of the vast power they hold. They should be punished for any violation they commit. But they should also be treated respectfully and not condemned without cause.

Susan Sarandon was wrong to participate in the Al Sharpton–led anticop demonstrations following the Diallo shooting. She should have given the system a chance to work. Every decent American felt terribly for the Diallo family. But besmirching a fine police force gained the country nothing. Absolutely nothing. In the end the system produced a trial. I pray the verdict was a fair one. But to people like Al Sharpton, only the conviction of the four cops would have been fair. That's the only outcome they would accept quietly. What explains that kind of attitude? Is it reasonable in the context of past abuses by police in the black communities? In an attempt to find out just what kind of man is fueling the "us against them" attitude that has taken deep root among many black Americans, the No Spin Zone beckoned to the Reverend Al Sharpton.

CHAPTER SEVEN

You Can Call Me Al

ISSUE 7: Boycotting for dollars
THE OPPONENT: Alfred Charles Sharpton, Jr.

O'REILLY: Look at how many African Americans get entry-level jobs at Burger King. You're hurting all those people.

SHARPTON: Why should we be happy getting entry-level jobs?

O'REILLY: Because sixteen-year-olds need them.

On the night of December 19, 1986, Michael Griffith, Cedric Sandiford, and Timothy Grimes found themselves stranded in the Howard Beach section of Queens, New York, when their car broke down. This was no easy Triple A call. These three black men from Brooklyn found themselves in a very close-knit, all-white, principally Italian neighborhood after dark. This was the home turf of mobster John Gotti and hundreds of Gotti wanna-bes. People who would say stuff to a reporter like "We see a black in high-top sneakers, we take him up to the roof and hang him over the side. Maybe we drop him, maybe we don't. Either way he don't come back."

The prevailing sentiment was that blacks were not wanted in Howard Beach, that they had no business being there anytime.

To make matters worse that night in 1986, the three young black men had exchanged insults with some Howard Beach locals shortly after their car died. The blacks left the car and went into a pizza joint. Upon leaving, they were attacked by a dozen white men, some of whom had baseball bats. Michael Griffith fled but was killed by a car as he ran across a busy highway. He was twenty-three. Cedric Sandiford was badly beaten. Timothy Grimes ran for his life and escaped relatively unharmed.

Subsequently, six of the attackers were convicted. But in the intervening months emotions ran high throughout New York City. No question but this was a bias attack of the worst kind. Revenge hung in the air like fog over a chilly lake.

The Reverend Al Sharpton took full advantage of the aggrieved climate and began leading a series of protest marches around the city, where slogans like "Howard Beach, have you heard? This is not Johannesburg" cut through the cold winter air.

As an ABC News correspondent at the time, I was assigned to cover perhaps the most intense demonstration, a march through Howard Beach on a Saturday afternoon. Sharpton, seeking national publicity, had decided to lead his followers, mostly black, back to the killing ground. He knew that on a Saturday most residents would be home. Hundreds of police officers lined up to prevent the expected mob violence. Sharpton was putting people in harm's way—no question about it.

Dressed in a polyester tracksuit with a heavy gold medallion hanging from his neck, Sharpton led the march looking more like a backup singer for James Brown than a man of the cloth. He chanted loudly but avoided any personal remarks directed at the hostile crowd of onlookers.

I suspected that the national media, which had not so far been taking Sharpton seriously, were making a mistake. This man had an agenda and was very much in control of the coverage of the situation. Previously, he'd been caught on audiotape ranting about "homos" and "white devils." His public rhetoric had often been crude and racially charged.

But on this day he was staying cleverly "on message." He made himself available for all interviewers and argued that the death of Michael Griffith spotlighted the prevailing injustice blacks face all across America. It was bunk. Howard Beach was an anomaly, an isolated place firmly rooted in the 1940s, but most Americans did not know that.

Sharpton's setup worked. Angry white bigots screamed racial insults and the reverend absorbed them silently. He looked heroic to many in the black community and to some whites as well. Sharpton had arrived and I was there to see it.

Fast-forward to the year 2000. Al Sharpton has traded the tracksuits for expensive three-button business suits and has become the nation's second most visible black spokesman after Jesse Jackson. Sharpton no longer looks like a lounge singer. Now he looks like an executive, which of course he is.

Moreover, taking his cue from Jackson, Sharpton runs an entity called the National Action Network, NAN, headquartered on Madison Avenue and 125th Street in Harlem. The energetic reverend also heads the Madison Avenue Initiative, with an office on the forty-second floor of the Empire State Building in mid-Manhattan. NAN, according to an article in the *Nation* by Scott Sherman, has a staff of twelve and an annual budget of $1.5 million.

The money comes from fund-raisers and donors like boxing promoter Don King, who wrote a check for $150,000.

NAN, also known as the House of Justice, picks up most expenses for the Sharpton family, including his extensive wardrobe, in the form of so-called love offerings. In other words, Sharpton lives comfortably without having to declare an income—a tax dodge widely used in the world of religion-based activism. This arrangement was especially convenient for Sharpton in 1998, when a civil court ordered him to fork over a $65,000 damage award to former assistant district attorney Steven Pagones for defamation in the notorious Tawana Brawley case. Sharpton claimed he had no personal funds to pay up. Finally, in June 2001, a group of his supporters did pay Pagones $87,000—the original judgment plus interest. Al did not have to open his wallet.

It is a mistake to not take Al Sharpton seriously. Ordained at age ten (that's right, ten) as a Pentecostal minister in Brooklyn, Sharpton has evolved into a savvy racial player. He was trained by the master, Jesse Jackson, who appointed Sharpton to a leadership position in Jackson's Operation Breadbasket in 1969. That operation organized boycotts of supermarkets and other retailers that did not conform to Jackson's hiring vision.

Here's how this particular shakedown game works: Jackson or Sharpton or some other operative will approach a business and threaten some public action like a demonstration or a boycott unless a certain demand is met. For example, the business will be "encouraged" to hire "consultants" who will offer "suggestions" for hiring minority contractors and employees. Are you surprised to hear that the "consultants" are often friends of the reverends— friends who donate large sums of money to their enterprises? Are you surprised that many of the minority contractors hired are also close to the reverends? I didn't think so.

This lucrative game, still thriving today, has been very profitable. Jackson in particular has developed a multimillion-dollar gravy train doing business with huge corporations like Texaco and Coca-Cola.

But in the year 2000 I was more interested in Al Sharpton's threatened boycott against all Burger King franchises in New York City. As I said to the reverend at one point, "I think boycotting is un-American; I don't believe in it." But he insisted that his boycott would produce more minority ownership in the fast-food chain, since only one franchise within the city limits was owned by an African American. This was puzzling because the Burger King Corporation had been supporting Al's pal Jesse Jackson and his organizations for twenty years, publicly admitting to having donated more than a half million dollars. How could B.K. be racist?

To his credit, Al Sharpton traveled to a place where Jesse Jackson fears to tread. Sharpton entered the No Spin Zone looking razor-sharp, his suit neatly pressed, his trademark long hair slicked back.

Naturally, Sharpton knew the Zone was not going to be "Al friendly," but he took the fire, readily made eye contact throughout the interview, and seemed to relish the intellectual joust. Was he right to threaten Burger King? You decide . . .

O'REILLY: Let me read you something from the *New Republic* magazine. "Last month, Jesse Jackson sent Al Sharpton a stiff letter warning that a boycott of Burger King might be counterproductive, since it could harm more than a hundred black and brown franchises employing more than eight thousand people. The boycott, Jackson says, would be premature." What is your response?

SHARPTON: My response is that in New York where the boycott is now—we haven't gone national yet—there's only one black owner. Our action isn't hurting black franchisers because we're not boycotting nationally yet.

O'REILLY: Did Jackson tell you to knock it off?

SHARPTON: Well, we talked after I got his letter, but I think *The New Republic* is just trying to pit him against me.

O'REILLY: Is it true that Burger King has been backing Rainbow/PUSH with an estimated $500,000?

SHARPTON: Burger King and the PUSH organization had a situation they worked out many years ago and it has caused millions of dollars to go into the black community.

O'REILLY: Do you think Burger King bought Jackson?

SHARPTON: No. Absolutely, I don't. They should have given 5 million bucks for what they're doing in the community and what Burger King has taken out of the community. If all they gave was $500,000, we should have a national boycott against them just for that.

O'REILLY: Wait a minute. Burger King doesn't owe you guys anything at all.

SHARPTON: Then we shouldn't consume there. That's all. It's go where the people respect you.

O'REILLY: You don't have to boycott. Just advertise your disenchantment.

SHARPTON: What you call advertising, I call boycotting.

O'REILLY: Look at how many African Americans get entry-level jobs at Burger King. You're hurting all those people.

SHARPTON: Why should we be happy getting entry-level jobs?

O'REILLY: Because sixteen-year-olds need them.

SHARPTON: But they also need promotions and we need to have public relations firms that can do service contracts. There are lots of things we need.

O'REILLY: Apparently, Jesse Jackson and other Americans feel that you're hurting entry-level youth by hurting the Burger King company, which is 15 percent minority-owned. And blacks comprise 13 percent of the country. Sounds like the company is right on the mark.

SHARPTON: No, Burger King is a problem. If you're going to take millions of dollars out of a community, the community ought to say, "We will shop with those that respect us best."

So there it is. Both Al Sharpton and Jesse Jackson have set themselves up as the overseers of inner-city commerce, champions of minority economic participation. Play it their way or pay a price. A steep price. This kind of economic pressure brings in an enormous amount of money from black-owned companies that donate to Sharpton and Jackson in the hope that the reverends will get them business. It is entirely legal and immensely profitable, although the two may now be stepping on each other's toes in the Burger King situation.

Some call it racial hustling, others say it is necessary for minorities to get their fair share. I believe Martin Luther King, Jr., would be appalled. He had a dream, not a hustle. He talked about sitting down together, not elbowing each other aside.

Americans of all colors would listen more seriously to Al Sharpton if, as I said to him, he becomes "an equal opportunity protester," representing all Americans who need justice. Race-driven agendas are obvious and exclusionary. Americans of good faith reject that. Sharpton and Jackson don't care, I believe, because there is money and power in the divisive role they play. And if you want even more evidence, the Reverend Al and I had one more go-around shortly after a national study revealed that 63 percent of black fourth graders attending public schools *can't read*. That is an astounding and disturbing statistic. Yet no demonstrations were led by the Reverends Sharpton and Jackson. I called Sharpton on it.

O'REILLY: Where are you and Jesse Jackson? I figured you would be out there with signs demonstrating in front of the Department of Education. Where are you guys?

SHARPTON: First, we must deal with the fact that the educational policy in terms of everything from classroom size to teacher performance needs to be dealt with.

O'REILLY: Fine. Why aren't you guys on the streets?

SHARPTON: John Ashcroft ought to be dealing with the waste and fraud.

O'REILLY: You're dodging the question.

SHARPTON: No. You're dodging the question.

O'REILLY: Whenever there's a black-white controversy you guys are there. You are not there on this issue. You are not visible and you have not mobilized.

SHARPTON: I think that is not true. We have spent a lot of time on educational issues.

O'REILLY: That shocking statistic about black fourth graders has been out for three weeks. No visible protest by you.

SHARPTON: I was in Sudan and in Puerto Rico.

O'REILLY: Come on. Sixty-three percent of black fourth graders can't read.

SHARPTON: I challenge you, O'Reilly, to come out of the studio and demonstrate with me. What is so strange is that the great O'Reilly is not saying, "Mr. Bush, what are you going to do?" You're asking Jesse Jackson and Al Sharpton. We're not the president.

O'REILLY: The way I see it—and I could be wrong—is that you guys will run out and polarize, but when it comes to really important issues like this, you disappear.

SHARPTON: Tell George Bush he needs to deal with this. We will certainly be telling him.

O'REILLY: And when you do, Reverend, we'll be right there covering it.

When the interview ended and the camera was off, Al Sharpton stood up, looked me in the eye, shook my hand, and said, "You're right about this one." I believe that is more than Jesse Jackson will ever say.

CHAPTER EIGHT

Jesse's World

ISSUE 8: Show us the money

THE OPPONENTS: Jesse Jackson and his supporters

SHELDON COHEN (former IRS commissioner): If the IRS were properly funded and was auditing the returns it ought to audit, which it's not, it would look at this [Jackson's Citizenship Education Fund] return . . .

O'REILLY: I'll tell you, Mr. Cohen, I'm not accusing anyone of anything, but this is why the bandits are getting away with it. They know you guys don't care. They know you're not going to do anything about it.

On March 8, 2001, a cool, windy day in Chicago, the Reverend Jesse Jackson stood behind a podium speaking to a group of black journalists. Spurred by reports on my program and follow-up articles in both Chicago newspapers, the journalists had asked to hear Jackson's explanation of payments made to Karin L. Stanford, through his tax-exempt charitable organization the Citizenship Education Fund. Ms. Stanford, until recently the executive director of CEF, was also Jackson's mistress and the mother of his twenty-month-old daughter.

Jackson at first acted as if he welcomed the opportunity to explain the situation.

"What you are asking me now is investigative journalism," he said. "And I don't mind because we are going to pass any test you all set up. Our books will stand the test. What we do, how we do it—we can agree or disagree, but we can handle investigative journalism."

But then Jesse Jackson drew a fine philosophical distinction—and you will soon see why—between the responsible scribes before him and newshounds like your humble correspondent. Said Jackson: "But when you got a combination in these times of pay-for-check journalism glorified by Fox or by [Rupert] Murdoch with a decided political agenda, that's a little different. And when O'Reilly gets a raise and ratings off your life, then it becomes something different."

Yep, the guy doesn't like me. Worse, he's called me "a right-wing extremist" bent on destroying all the good work he's accomplished in his more than three decades on the national civil rights scene. From conversations and confrontations with his defenders, I gather that he's convinced I'm on some sort of jihad against him and everything for which he stands.

Back in 1999 my staff and I kept hearing that the reverend might be using tax-exempt funds to pay off personal obligations. If true, that was one heck of a story, and we're in the news business, right? To find out the truth, I assigned producer Heath Kern to look into the situation.

The obvious place to start was the tax returns of Jackson's Citizenship Education Fund and his People United to Save Humanity (PUSH). Since both organizations are tax-exempt, their books should be open to the public. But when Ms. Kern approached Jackson's staff about examining the returns, she was told they were "none of your business."

Not a good answer to aggressive journalists.

For more than a year we pressured the authorities in Illinois for copies of the CEF returns. Finally, we were provided with the documents filed by the group for 1998 and 1999. That's how we got the first glimpse of a "mistake" that blew up into a major news story and inspired others to look into the situation as well.

It all began with the neatly typed word "None." That was the word on the line where Jackson's people were supposed to list any staffers who were paid more than $50,000 a year.

The truth is, Karin Stanford received between $64,000 and $120,000 as the D.C.-based CEF executive director in 1999 (it seems that every time Jackson's people address the issue the figure changes). And four other people were paid more than $50,000 that year. After the story broke, Billy R. Owens, the newly hired chief financial officer of Jackson's organizations (at a reported annual salary of $137,000), explained to the *Chicago Tribune* that he was "unsure" why Stanford and the others were not listed and that the returns would "probably" have to be amended to reflect the truth of the matter. (As you will see below, another Jackson adherent offered a similar reaction when trying to spin in the No Spin Zone.)

By the way, Jackson hired Owens soon after *The O'Reilly Factor* started knocking on his door, but that may just be a coincidence. The official explanation for Owens's employment was the need for improved management, and you can hardly disagree with that. For example, the tax returns show that the Citizenship Education Fund collected a whopping $12 million in donations over that two-year period, but spent less than 1 percent of the money on actual education. As of this writing, Jackson has not specifically reported how the rest of the money was spent.

We also learned that in addition to paying Ms. Stanford big bucks in salary, the CEF paid her $35,000 to move *away* from her job in Washington after she gave two days' notice and resigned her position. This was about the time she became pregnant with Jackson's child.

Jackson himself is paid $120,000 a year by his tax-exempt organizations and racked up an incredible $614,000 in travel expenses in the year 2000 (we are still waiting to see the itemization) out of $1.3 million in travel for the entire staff. Evidently, the Democratic Party reimbursed him $450,000 for traveling—a very questionable transaction in light of his tax-exempt status, which requires that all activities be nonpartisan.

To be fair, the reverend long ago admitted that he has taken no vow of poverty. A millionaire, he puts his annual gross pay north of $400,000. He owns three homes, often travels first-class, and mostly stays in the best hotels. According to *Chicago Sun-Times* columnist Mary Mitchell, his CNN talk show (recently canceled) paid him $260,000 annually, and he averages another $50,000 in speaking fees (his agent for speeches is his wife, Jacqueline). Jackson also picks up cash doing freelance projects. For example, my former employer, King World, paid him more than $200,000 for a series of interviews.

Jackson's empire, reportedly with $17 million on hand in the year 2000, consists of four distinct but interconnected organizations: PUSH, the Citizenship Education Fund (CEF), PUSH for Excellence, and the Rainbow/PUSH Coalition. CEF, the largest, has been pledged some $4 million by GTE, Bell Atlantic, Viacom, AT&T, and SBC-Ameritech. Reportedly, about one hundred people work for the four organizations; their average salary is about $42,000. In addition, Jackson runs an annual Wall Street Project that attracts big shots from all walks of life. Contributions to Jackson flow at this event.

✳

As Clint Eastwood might put it: "The question you should be asking yourself is, where *is* the IRS?" What could the feared tax guys be thinking? Despite more red flags than a Havana May Day parade and Jackson's history of money chaos, the IRS has given him a pass. Let's look at the record.

- In 1979 government auditors questioned $1.7 million that Operation PUSH spent in grants from the Carter administration. Jackson was forced to repay half a million dollars to Uncle Sam—that means to us the taxpayers. The American Institute for Research found in a government-funded study that the program the grants funded could not point to any appreciable accomplishments.

- In another case, Department of Education auditors contended that PUSH had failed to account for $1.2 million in grants. The feds, you will be happy to hear, disbursed no more monies to Jackson's organizations after that.

- The Federal Election Commission (FEC) had problems with money flowing to Jackson's two presidential campaigns. The 1984 campaign, according to the commission's auditors, "underreported" receipts by $826,000 and expenditures by more than $1 million. After an extensive investigation, the campaign was fined $13,000 for violations of reporting rules. Four years later, Jackson's campaign reporting practices had not noticeably improved. The 1988 effort was fined a record $150,000 civil judgment, even after they agreed to repay $122,000 of the taxpayer subsidies.

These are just the highlights . . . yet the IRS apparently remains satisfied that Jackson's organizations have their books in good order. CFO Owens has confirmed that the powerful tax agency *has not contacted him*. In fact, the IRS has not seen fit to audit Jackson's returns in twelve years.

But now there is some pressure. A complaint has been filed with the IRS by the National Legal and Policy Center, a conservative group, in regard to the Citizenship Education Fund's activities. Another complaint has been filed with the FEC by the American Conservative Union, which is disturbed by the reimbursement of Jackson's travel expenses by the Democratic Party.

Still, the IRS is silent. Is it timidity? Well, nobody in that buttoned-up organization would venture into the No Spin Zone, but former IRS commissioner Sheldon Cohen did accept my invitation to visit the Zone. It is safe to say he will remember the experience.

COHEN: I suspect the IRS will take a look [at Jackson's books].
O'REILLY: You suspect it would? You would think it would! This Citizenship Education Fund raised $12 million in two years and $47,000 goes to education. Is that not a red flag for the IRS?

COHEN: I don't know what they spent the rest of the money for.

O'REILLY: Let me read you some other parts of the CEF return. $1,307,393 on consultants? Isn't that a lot of money for consultants?

COHEN: You and I both suspect that's not proper, but on the face of it, that doesn't mean it's not proper. So, for example, suppose those consultants were studying the early childhood education for poor kids. If the studies are pursuant to the educational goals of the foundation, that would be all right . . .

O'REILLY: More than a million to consultants and the return doesn't say who the consultants are.

COHEN: The consultants could or could not be proper—no tax return shows the detail.

O'REILLY: When I fill out my tax return and list charitable donations, I have to name the charities and how much I gave them. Are you telling me that Reverend Jackson doesn't have to do the same thing?

COHEN: I am saying that a tax-exempt organization has to supply very little detail. They are not required to do it.

O'REILLY: So what you are saying is that he [Jackson] doesn't have to tell us who the consultants are that were paid more than a million tax-exempt dollars. But if the IRS goes in and asks, then he has to tell.

COHEN: Exactly right.

O'REILLY: But at this point the IRS isn't asking despite all these expenditures that don't look right.

COHEN: If the IRS were properly funded and was auditing the returns it ought to audit, which it's not, it would look at this [Jackson's CEF] return amongst many others . . .

O'REILLY: I'll tell you, Mr. Cohen, I'm not accusing anyone of anything, but this is why the bandits are getting away with it. They know you guys don't care. They know you're not going to do anything about it.

COHEN: Believe me, the people at the IRS care.

O'REILLY: I don't believe it for a second, Mr. Cohen, and I don't think anybody who has seen our investigation believes you either. But we appreciate your time.

I was tough on Sheldon Cohen, maybe too tough. The situation is not his fault, but he felt the need to defend the IRS and I felt the need to call him on that. You can decide if I went over the line.

The consultant deal is of key importance in the Jackson case. For years various people have said that one of Jesse Jackson's most lucrative money-raising techniques is to pressure large corporations to improve minority hiring and contracting by hiring specific "consultants" that he recommends. "Minority suppliers," one company official explained to me on the air, "is a catchword for some of [Jackson's] friends who want to get contracts." If the lucky designees are hired, the story goes, then they're likely to show their gratitude by donating to a Jackson organization.

Allegedly, in other words, it's quid pro quo all over the place, and it has reportedly been going on for quite some time. In May 1988 *The New Republic*, hardly part of the vast right-wing conspiracy, ran an article entitled "Jesse's Business: A Shakedown Racket?" The answer in the article is somewhat mixed, but one quote stands out. Conservative African American publisher Hurley Green opined, "Any time Jesse shows up now, it's going to cost you."

For years even the largest, most powerful companies that have dealt with Jackson have remained silent. Why? Because even a multibillion-dollar corporation that sells to consumers is extremely vulnerable to the threat of a boycott or demonstration or bad press, and everyone in corporate America knows that.

Most such companies erect a wall of "no comment" around their dealings with Jesse Jackson. They know he can inflict pain. But walls eventually crumble, and the Rainbow Wall of Silence is no exception. People are beginning to speak out.

For example, T. J. Rogers, president of Cypress Semiconductor, publicly criticized Jesse Jackson for trying to intimidate him into doing business with Jackson's associates. And Tom Roeser, a former vice president of the Quaker Oats Company, entered the No Spin Zone with an amazing tale centered upon the pancake icon Aunt Jemima. Roeser would say frankly that Jackson's behavior "had all the charm of a vintage Mafioso."

Now, millions of Americans have grown up with the Aunt Jemima figure, a smiling, plump black woman wearing an apron and bandana. In the early 1970s Quaker Oats was selling a ton of Aunt Jemima pancake mix. In other words, product and company were highly profitable—and highly visible. A recipe, you might say, for Jesse Jackson's money zone.

Tom Roeser asserted on *The O'Reilly Factor* TV program that the Reverend Jackson threatened Quaker Oats with a boycott if the company didn't modify what Jackson saw as a racial stereotype. When the company agreed to sit down with Jackson and his cohorts in Manhattan to discuss the issue, Roeser chaired the Quaker Oats negotiating team. As you will see, he did not shy away from very frank language.

O'REILLY: Some people saw a heavyset black woman wearing a bandana and thought it was stereotypical. Did they have a point?

ROESER: No, they didn't, because Aunt Jemima was a fictional character. She's no more a stereotype than, say, the Quaker Man, who wears white curls and hearkens back to William Penn. And by the time Jesse Jackson approached, Aunt Jemima had already been modified to represent a kind of suburban, upscale African American woman. Instead of the bandana, we had a headband. She slimmed down.

O'REILLY: All right. Jesse Jackson says he has a problem with Aunt Jemima. Was that the reason for the meeting?

ROESER: That's correct. Jackson's point was to extort—and I use that word advisedly—a tithe as a result of threatening a boycott of Quaker Oats. And he did it in subtle ways.

O'REILLY: Walk me through it.

ROESER: Well, Jackson says he wants to negotiate with us on a number of things. Certainly minority suppliers, which is a catchword for some of their friends who want to get contracts. Certainly employment. That's okay, although there was a federal program in line for employment. Also, blacks on the board, and also foundation gifts.

O'REILLY: Blacks make up about 13 percent of the American population. Did Quaker Oats have 13 percent black employment?

ROESER: It was lower.

O'REILLY: So Jackson had a point. You guys should have had more minority workers.

ROESER: Well, he did have a point. But we were on the way toward that goal.

O'REILLY: So you took his point.

ROESER: The point, Bill, is that we had no objection to meeting with Jackson, but we did object to what I thought was an extortionate type of activity. I'm paraphrasing here. He says, "We would hate to jeopardize your company. For example, if there were a picket line thrown around the headquarters of the company, that might hurt. We don't want to do that." It had all the charm of a vintage Mafioso.

O'REILLY: What did you guys do?

ROESER: Well, what we did say is that we would not sign a covenant. He wanted to sign a covenant with us. We gave him some money, but it wasn't a large amount. Some of it went to black community organizations, some to his suppliers. We made certain concessions to him. All of them under threat.

O'REILLY: So Jackson won. He beat you.

ROESER: No, he didn't beat us, because we didn't sign the covenant. We paid him a lot of money in terms of suppliers but he wanted us to dump the Aunt Jemima brand and we didn't.

The list of companies that Jesse Jackson has done "business" with is staggering. Corporate sponsors for his Wall Street Project donate millions to his organizations. Consider the following, which are only a few of many examples:

1. Texaco. To stroke Jackson, the giant oil corporation agreed to spend $1 billion over five years with minority-controlled businesses and also dole out $140 million to compensate minorities already on the payroll. Texaco was acting after tapes of supposedly racist comments by executives were made public, but the story turned out to be dubious. Texaco's dealings with Jackson, however, were anything but dubious; they cost the company a bundle.

2. Anheuser-Busch. Even though leaders of the black community in the giant beer company's headquarters town, St. Louis, objected to his actions, Jesse Jackson made his

usual demands in the '80s. One result: His sons Yusef and Jonathan, twenty-eight and thirty-two years old at the time, were given 90 percent ownership of River North, a Busch distributorship in Chicago with an annual revenue of $28 million. The Jackson kids had no previous beverage experience.

3. AT&T. Through Jackson's Wall Street Project, AT&T agreed to broker about $1 billion in bonds using the minority-owned Blaylock & Partners Group. Of course that firm is close to Jesse Jackson and contributes generously to his concerns.

There are plenty more, with companies like Merrill Lynch, Travelers Insurance, Goldman Sachs, and Prudential Insurance all writing large checks to Jackson's organizations. As mentioned in the preceding chapter, Jackson's financial dealings with Burger King caused a ruckus between him and Al Sharpton. But that's unusual. The money flow usually benefits all who are friendly with Jackson, and what goes around comes around. If you know what I mean.

And powerful politicians are also not above making deals with the Reverend Jackson. Governor George Ryan of Illinois was taking a verbal pounding from Jackson over a variety of issues when he finally gave in and struck a deal. Jackson's Operation PUSH would receive a one-year contract and $763,000 to help the state of Illinois enroll poor children in a federally funded health insurance program called KidCare. PUSH's mission was to convince parents to fill out the forms necessary for the state to pay for health insurance. It was as simple as that.

After the deal was sealed and the money flow assured, Jackson's criticism of Governor Ryan ceased. And, on paper, KidCare seemed to be a perfect match for PUSH, an organization set up to help the poor. But according to reporting done by the *Chicago Sun-Times*, in the first seven months of the one-year contract, Operation PUSH only signed up 151 families for KidCare. That's almost 800,000 taxpayer bucks spent and 151 families reached. You do the math.

The most important question is, why did Operation PUSH fail to sign up more families for this program? There's no question that thousands of Illinois families continue to lack health insurance, and KidCare was designed to combat that. How many children did not receive proper medical treatment because their parents didn't sign up for KidCare?

Reverend Jackson has not seen fit to answer that question or explain the low numbers of people his group signed up for KidCare. Jackson will say only that "we are public service, not perfect service." And to many Americans, that bit of rhetoric is not enough to prevent the thought that KidCare turned into KidCon.

Because of the KidCare fiasco, the mistress payment situation, and a variety of other unanswered questions, Jesse Jackson would not dare enter the No Spin Zone despite having been asked scores of times. So I have had to settle for Jackson's supporters.

His primary defender has been attorney Lewis Myers, who works directly for him. Myers is a smart, engaging fellow and he knew the heat from the *Factor*'s investigation was getting to the volcanic level in March of 2001. Counselor Myers knew we had vetted the 1998 and 1999 Citizenship Education Fund tax returns. And he knew the returns did not look good.

MYERS: First of all, I think that any organization that uses public funds, Bill, is a legitimate target for an investigation. We don't have a problem with it. Our records have been very public. The problem comes in when the investigation takes a turn where there are obvious biases and where there are things that question the integrity of the investigator.

O'REILLY: *(laughs)* I guess that's my integrity. I would like to point out that it took us more than a year to get the Citizenship Education Fund tax returns—the ones where the mistress's salary wasn't listed. You weren't forthcoming in the beginning.

MYERS: We weren't forthcoming because we didn't feel that your investigation and the things that you were requiring and that you had been saying on this program lent itself to wanting to cooperate with somebody who obviously held a bias—

O'REILLY: And what bias do I have?

MYERS: Let me say this, Bill. We reviewed your request and I don't have a problem in opening the books, but I do have a problem when people have what I consider to be an insincere desire—

O'REILLY: Let's spell it out, Counselor. Here I am. What's my bias? What am I trying to do?

MYERS: Let me be very straight. For the last year and a half you have used this program and the national forum you have to not only trash Jesse Jackson, to trash Rainbow/PUSH, to trash the good deeds and the good works that we have done—

O'REILLY: Wait a minute, Counselor. That's a pretty provocative charge. Can you give me one example of what I've said that's trashed any good deed that you've done?

MYERS: I could probably be here for the next five years.

O'REILLY: Just one example, Counselor.

MYERS: You come on TV and you bring on four or five anti-

Jackson commentators before we have a chance to make our presentation to the public.

O'REILLY: Not true. We've had just as many pro-Jackson as anti-Jackson people on the *Factor*. Is that all you've got?

MYERS: You've attacked Jesse Jackson personally?

O'REILLY: How?

MYERS: Through your show, your commentary, the language you've used—

O'REILLY: Just give me one example.

MYERS: Just take the tax situation. There has been nothing illegal about how we've filed our IRS claims.

O'REILLY: That's not personal. That's business.

MYERS: Let me give you something concrete. You put two individuals on your program—not only did they trash us, they trashed us with bias and you were leading them on.

O'REILLY: I don't know what you're talking about, Counselor. But I will tell you this. It took us a year and a half to get Citizenship Education Fund records for '98, '99. When we got them, there was nobody listed making more than $50,000 a year when Ms. Stanford was making $120,000.

MYERS: Let me respond to that. Mr. Billy Owens, who is our chief financial officer, came before the world and said a mistake had been made.

O'REILLY: A mistake.

MYERS: We realized a mistake had been made.

O'REILLY: All right, Counselor. In an organization that has what, a dozen employees? A mistake of that magnitude was made for two years running. I'll be like the Ghostbusters—I'm ready to believe you.

MYERS: No, no, no, Bill, that's a misstatement. She wasn't the only person who was making more than $50,000. We had at least five people.

O'REILLY: That just compounds the mistake five times!

MYERS: The fact is we did not violate any law.

O'REILLY: I'm not saying what you did was illegal. But I am saying that we have questions Jesse Jackson will not answer. Now I'm going to issue you a challenge, Counselor. You have said that I am biased and unfair. I will give you and Jesse Jackson a full hour to explain the situation. Two against one, Counselor, come in here and set the record straight.

MYERS: Bill, I wouldn't abuse you like that. I understand your challenge, but I won't take you up on it.

Take me up on it? Why should he, if his boss has both the IRS and the state of Illinois tucked away in his pocket? A skeptical reporter is a minor annoyance if the fix is in at those levels.

Myers didn't exactly play the race card, but he came close. What bias do I have against Reverend Jackson? You judge. I am perfectly willing to grant that he has done some positive and remarkable things in his life. He has brought attention to the legitimate complaints of racial minorities in the corporate world and has championed the underdog with astounding energy. But it is my opinion that somewhere along the way Jackson began to exploit the racial situation for his own benefit. Whether it is the addiction of money and women, or something else, he has gone down the wrong path. His self-promotion and thinly veiled threats have brought him riches and arrogance.

Except for the connection to tax-exempt funds, I don't care about his mistress or his private life. I have a baby around the age of Jackson's out-of-wedlock child, so I feel for the little girl. But I don't question Jackson's right to promote his ideology or causes.

As with all other Americans, he is entitled to his opinion and advocacy.

But he is *not* entitled to use my money to further his personal and political agenda. He is *not* entitled to use tax-exempt funds to pay women to keep quiet about personal issues that involve him. He's also *not* entitled to use tax-exempt funds to support any efforts to extort money from companies and divert contracts and franchises to his friends and family.

Did Jackson actually do any or all of those things? Well, I don't have subpoena powers, so I can't get to the bottom of it all. The authorities, who could do so, are clearly afraid to go searching for the truth—as they are required to do as guardians of the public trust.

Nor has the elite media ventured anywhere near this potential land mine. It's been the *Factor* and the Chicago papers leading the way. The networks and big liberal papers were MIA.

I know why and so do you, but let's hear it from someone who's been at the center of the action. Delmarie Cobb, a former reporter, was the reverend's traveling press secretary in 1988. Since that time she has been quiet about Jackson's activities—but she did agree to enter the No Spin Zone shortly after Jackson held a press conference during which he attacked me.

Attractive and soft-spoken, Ms. Cobb memorably said, before the following excerpt, that "the media and Jesse Jackson have been dance partners for a very long time . . . and now Jesse Jackson or one of the partners has made a misstep. So now all of the partners are on their own."

What does that mean exactly? Here it comes.

O'REILLY: Why won't you see an investigation of Jesse Jackson on the network newscasts?

COBB: For years the media was afraid.

O'REILLY: Why are they afraid?

COBB: They are afraid to do any close investigating because they don't want to be called racist.

O'REILLY: That took a lot of guts to say, Ms. Cobb.

COBB: Thank you.

Later, Delmarie Cobb would be quoted in the *New York Times* as saying about Jackson, "What he did was put everything at risk by brazen, hypocritical and reckless behavior." In a similar vein, Peter Flaherty, president of the National Legal and Policy Center, wrote in the *Detroit News*, "Until now, an informal but enforced silence has existed about what has been obvious to millions of Americans for years—namely, that Jesse Jackson came to do good but instead did very well."

What happens next? What more will come out about Jesse Jackson? Will he keep his power and prominence?

As of this writing, the story is getting murkier. There is a kind of media civil war going on. In the middle of all his controversies, Jackson was named Newsmaker of the Year by the National Newspaper Publishing Association. This professional trade association boasts a membership of 210 black publications across the country. Yes, the award was intended as an honor.

And you haven't forgotten the reverend's charitable defense of the womanizing Bill Clinton, have you? Far down the list of questionable pardons showered on the unworthy by the departing President Clinton was former Chicago congressman Mel Reynolds. His six-and-a-half-year federal sentence for bank fraud, wire fraud, and lying to the Federal Election Commission, which he was serving concurrently with a five-year stretch for having sex with a minor and soliciting child pornography, was commuted. The forgiving Jesse Jackson speedily named Reynolds a paid consultant on prison reform for the Rainbow/PUSH Coalition. As they say, you can't make this stuff up.

But I am confident that if Mr. Reynolds makes more than $50,000 tax-exempt, it will appear on the newly mistake-free tax forms that the reverend will undoubtedly be filing. As he is now saying: "Our books will stand the test."

Well, they didn't stand the test of the No Spin Zone. But neither do many other things. And included among them is the legacy of Bill Clinton.

CHAPTER NINE

This Bill Is Past Due

ISSUE 9: The legacy of Bill Clinton

THE OPPONENT: James Carville, former Clinton campaign manager

CARVILLE: I told somebody—I said defending President Clinton is like being in the Mafia, you just can't get out of the thing. I'm like Michael Corleone. How do I get out of this business?

O'REILLY: Can I say just one thing? Really, this whole event has been worth it to hear James Carville admit he's been involved with organized crime for the past eight years!

There is no question in my mind that the presidency of Bill Clinton will go down in history as one of the most fascinating Oval Office adventures ever. The self-described "man from Hope," young and articulate, campaigned until he was hoarse and defeated a sitting president who was credited with winning the Persian Gulf

War. But from the very beginning, Mr. Clinton played right into the hands of his many enemies and was constantly under suspicion for playing fast and loose with the truth.

Early on, there were the ladies from Dolly Kyle Browning to Gennifer Flowers to Paula Jones and with heavy rumors about scores of others. Explanations from the Clinton spinners were never convincing. But these "bimbo eruptions" were soon knocked off the front pages by more important activities. Like an Alpine brook trickling at first downhill then growing into a raging river, the stories segued smoothly from Whitewater, to the White House travel office firings, to unauthorized FBI files showing up at 1600 Pennsylvania Avenue.

Because of this wealth of exposés, spinners began talking about "Clinton fatigue" during his first term. Few could have guessed that the hits would just keep on coming in Clinton's second term with the Monica Lewinsky impeachment, Chinese espionage, and hundreds of campaign finance violations linked to the poll-popular president. Again and again, Clinton escaped just in the nick of time, all the while smiling and shaking his head. He was totally innocent of any and all wrongdoing. Those damn right-wingers just couldn't stop manufacturing stuff.

Toward the end of his tenure, when the worst seemed to be over for Mr. Clinton, there was the sideshow of the Elián González affair and then, topping things off with a spectacular finale, the fiasco of the midnight pardons—inappropriate, suspicious, and very possibly bought.

The pardons may have proved what some eyewitnesses had privately reported during Mr. Clinton's presidential tenure—that in public he was an engaging, self-confident fellow but behind the scenes he could be morose and incredibly arrogant. Addicted to constant polling, he had seen his public support remain historically strong, even as the talking heads in Washington and New York called for his resignation. But the on-fire economy sedated public opinion, and at least a third of Americans said they admired the man, sticking by him even today despite the crassness of his behavior in office.

Perhaps I made a mistake during my ongoing analysis of President Clinton. I took him *personally*. You can feel the anger in this brief excerpt from my previous book *The O'Reilly Factor: The Good, the Bad, and the Completely Ridiculous in American Life:* "What a ridiculous waste! Full of promise, intelligence, and charisma, this man will go down in history alongside Warren Harding and Richard Nixon as the most corrupt presidents of the twentieth century. What a legacy for an Arkansas boy with a modest background who made it to the most powerful office in the world. It's not only ridiculous, it's pathetic."

I don't consider myself a Clinton hater because it was not his persona that I took exception to—it was his *behavior*. The guy *really* made me angry. When he looked in the eyes of PBS anchorman Jim Lehrer and denied having sex with Ms. Lewinsky, I almost believed him. My reporter's brain was humming. Nobody, I thought, could lie that brazenly on national television. It would be political suicide. Maybe he had been set up, just as his wife and other spinners were saying. The scenario was really getting interesting.

My doubt was short-lived and would never appear again when it came to Bill Clinton. The DNA evidence on Monica Lewinsky's dress put Clinton into a category of public dishonesty few politicians could survive. The world saw President Clinton for what he was: a bold liar. It didn't matter what he was lying about—he was lying. Any honest person should have been appalled that a sitting president of the United States would dare deceive his constituents so brazenly.

But millions of Americans were not appalled and some were even angry with people like me who came down hard on Clinton. Ideology and apathy ruled the day. Even the venerated Lehrer didn't call Clinton on the lie. When the president needed another friendly sit-down TV chat, he again chose Jim Lehrer. When I saw the meek anchorman avoid questioning Clinton on the fact that he had lied to his face, I lost all respect for Lehrer as a journalist.

The Lewinsky episode was particularly fascinating because it introduced an intriguing cultural fault line in 1990s America. On one side were Americans, including me, who expected, even demanded, that a president be an example of honesty and exemplary behavior. On the other side were Americans who didn't care about the president's "private life," even when his lies about sex undermined a court case. To these Americans, such tawdry behavior was excusable, as long as Mr. Clinton took the proper ideological positions and kept the economy strong.

The chief pettifogger and Energizer Bunny for the pro-Clinton forces was political strategist James Carville, whose official title was Senior Political Adviser to the President. Brilliant and fast-lipped, the native Louisianan tore through the Clinton opposition like an airboat through a bayou. Carville was a true believer—a man who was convinced Bill Clinton had the good of the regular, hardworking American on his mind.

After playing a significant role in Clinton's defeat of President Bush in 1992, the "Ragin' Cajun" became the point man against the vast right-wing conspiracy that all the Clintonistas believed would do anything to bring their man down. Carville's most successful strategy was to label all attacks on Clinton as "partisan," and he ate most of the press for breakfast. He intimidated, mocked, dismissed, and verbally abused them. They couldn't touch his most famous line: "It's only about sex." He was Bill and

Hillary Clinton's avenger and he was undefeated. (In fact, according to an account in Peter Baker's book *The Breach*, the First Lady asked Carville to race back from a trip to South America as impeachment heated up and said, "You just have to help us get through this. I don't know how we can get through this.")

Naturally, I desperately wanted to get Carville into the No Spin Zone. But he wouldn't play. He told the press that I had insulted his wife, Republican pundit Mary Matalin, by asking her to put him out of the house until he showed up on *The O'Reilly Factor*. I did, indeed, say that. But it was a jest and Carville knew it. As usual, though, he spun the press and avoided the *Factor*, choosing to face Russert, King, and Lauer but not your humble correspondent.

That is, until March 26, 2001. That's when former Clinton chief of staff Leon Panetta brought James Carville and Bill O'Reilly together at the Monterey, California, Civil Center. The event was a current-events discussion sponsored by Panetta's Political Institute. It would be taped by C-Span and Fox News and broadcast coast-to-coast. Some called it something akin to a pro wrestling contest. The event sold out within hours; the waiting list for tickets stretched into the thousands.

I had never met the fifty-seven-year-old Carville, who is busy these days giving speeches, advising overseas office seekers, and watching his two young kids (wife Mary Matalin is one of Vice President Cheney's close advisers and is often out of the house). So when Leon Panetta introduced us in his office, I was prepared for the worst. But unlike his public persona, Carville is a bit shy in person and certainly a gentleman. Trading quips with Panetta and sharing some personal background, we got along fine, even as we felt each other out intellectually.

Our public debate was also civil but much more intense. Although we kidded around backstage, once we were introduced to the crowd (evenly divided between Clintonites and anti-Clintonites), things got lively fast. Panetta did not waste any time getting to the heart of the matter.

PANETTA: Give me your summary of the Clinton legacy.

O'REILLY: Well, I think Americans are deeply divided about him. Personally, he's very likable and I admire the fact that he came from nothing and rose up to become the most powerful man in the world. But I think he is a corrupt individual. My reporting over the past six years indicates one after another after another example of walking the ethical line. He spent a tremendous amount of time doing things other than the people's business. I think he's a tragic guy.

CARVILLE: He's a good friend of mine, and he obviously made some mistakes. He paid for it and he'll have to pay in history. But I'll tell you this: We spent more money investigating Bill Clinton than we spent on TWA 800, the Unabomber, and the Oklahoma City bombing combined. I think Clinton is the smartest guy I've seen in politics or anywhere else. If you look at his record, he improved things almost everywhere. I think that's got to be part of his legacy.

O'REILLY: I'd like to rebut that. One of the reasons we spent so much money investigating President Clinton is that he did not cooperate in the investigations. He used his tremendous power to hire brilliant people like James Carville to defend him. And he had an attorney general who blocked investigations time after time. Her own agents testified to that. Janet Reno's own people said publicly—we can't investigate.

CARVILLE: Janet Reno started more independent counsels and more investigations than any other attorney general in history. And the truth is, after $100 million they caught him acting stupid with a young woman and lying about it and that's it. The Filegate investigation, the Travelgate investigation, the every other kind of thing you can imagine, and that's what they come up with? Nothing. All of that for nothing.

O'REILLY: In the thirties there was a guy named Al Capone, remember that name? Remember all the federal investigations into Al Capone? They got nothing. Finally, they nailed him on tax evasion. Because as all of us know, Al Capone really never did anything at all.

CARVILLE: I rest my case.

So ended round one about Bill Clinton. The conversation then turned to other subjects like the government entitlements (Carville likes them) and the ridiculous energy debacle in California (Carville has confidence in Democratic Governor Gray Davis). But it was not long before Clinton, like the Phoenix he is, rose up in conversation again.

PANETTA: What will Bill Clinton do with the rest of his life besides golf? Want to take a crack at that, James?

CARVILLE: I don't know. I always wind up talking about him. I told somebody—I said defending President Clinton is like being in the Mafia, you just can't get out of the thing. I'm like Michael Corleone. How do I get out of this business?

O'REILLY: Can I say just one thing? Really, this whole event has been worth it to hear James Carville admit he's been involved with organized crime for the past eight years!

That line brought down the house, but Carville was undeterred. He dusted himself off and got back up off the canvas, ever the true believer.

CARVILLE: I think I can say without fear of hesitation, equivocation, or reservation that Bill Clinton is the single most talented guy I've ever known. He'll do fine without my advice.

O'REILLY: James is right about that; Clinton is a brilliant man. But he's also a corrupt man, and unless Jesse Jackson can convince him to go straight, I don't have a lot of hope he's not going to be a corrupt guy in the future. By the way, James, why does Mr. Clinton *need* a guy like you?

CARVILLE: If you're running for president, you have spinners. Yeah, you do. I'll tell you exactly the advice I give. It's okay to have an opinion on everything. It's just not okay to render said opinion. There's some glory to the unspoken thought. We spend most of our time telling them what they can't say.

PANETTA: That's how you screw these guys up.

O'REILLY: Carville is a nice guy. I never met him before tonight. I used to think he was the devil, now I just think he's a demon. He's working himself up.

CARVILLE: Thanks for the compliment.

O'REILLY: You're welcome. But why *do* these guys need you? Why don't they just speak from the heart? We should have politicians that say what they believe, how they want to help, and how they will solve problems. That's what America needs.

The Monterey audience burst into applause in agreement with that point. The debate ended soon afterward. But let's go back to my suggestion: Wouldn't America be a better place if politicians didn't rely on spinners like James Carville? Wouldn't this country be healthier if we had leaders who rejected spin and simply told us what they believed and why they believed it? Damn the spin—full disclosure ahead.

That kind of approach, of course, would put the James

Carvilles of the world out of business. Then maybe Mr. Carville could turn his attention to problem-solving rather than problem-excusing.

At another point in the debate I said, "Call me naive, but I think most politicians want to get into public service for the right reasons, but then it goes haywire with the money and the advisers and the spinners and the calculators . . . Then it gets to a point where our leaders don't know what they think. If they think at all." (Ironically, James Carville's top ten advice tips to Democrats posted on his website include the following comment in No. 1 Run for Office: "You don't need some overpriced consultant to run your race." Unless, of course, you can't tell the truth on a dare and have more skeletons in your closet than Vincent Price.)

You can tell that I enjoyed skirmishing with the king of spin, James Carville. He is a very smart guy, and that joust is most likely the closest I'll ever get to debating Bill Clinton himself.

But if the ex-president won't step into the No Spin Zone, he should answer in some forum somewhere for his extremely questionable conduct while in office. It's a mistake, and an insult, for him to continue eluding questions that trouble so many of his former constituents. Clinton's candor bill is clearly overdue. He owes the country some straight talk.

As George W. Bush said once on my TV program, showing a witty side, "I think one of [Clinton's] statements was that he was going to have the cleanest administration ever—but he was forty-one presidents shy."

And speaking of President Bush, he did travel in a different dimension—he did enter the No Spin Zone.

CHAPTER TEN

Bush-Wacked

ISSUE 10: Capital punishment

THE OPPONENT: George W. Bush, president of the United States

BUSH: I can't justify the death penalty in terms of the New Testament. I'm going to justify it in terms of the law, and in terms of saving people's lives. I believe that the death penalty when administered surely, swiftly, and justly saves people's lives. I believe it sends a chilling signal that if you kill somebody in my state in the commission of a crime, there's going to be a consequence and you're not going to like it.

O'REILLY: So you might disagree with Jesus on this one? I don't believe he would be embracing the death penalty if he were here today. But I could be wrong.

President George W. Bush is not a dumb man. Nobody can graduate from Harvard Business School and be dumb. You can get *into*

Harvard by pulling some strings, but to get out with a diploma you have to negotiate some heavy academic seas. Senator Edward Kennedy was expelled from Harvard.

President Bush's problem is one that plagued Cool Hand Luke: "a failure to communicate." The president, quite simply, listens to too many spinners and tries to memorize what they tell him. The result is often an awkward presentation and verbiage that would confuse Norm Crosby (if you remember that comedian of yore, give yourself three no spin points). Bush's uneasiness with his prepared presentations also presents itself in the form of a smirk and, at times, a stare that would frighten a zombie.

My all-time favorite so far: When a journalist wrote that Bush suffers from dyslexia, the candidate retorted, "That lady who wrote that I had dyslexia? I never even interviewed her."

My first meeting with Mr. Bush took place at the Stony Brook campus of the State University of New York on March 3, 2000, just before the crucial Super Tuesday primaries. At that point, Bush was locked in a death dance with Senator John McCain and had to win the majority of the state primaries or McCain would leap into solid contention. So George W. Bush was campaigning in unfriendly territory, the liberal state of New York, and contemplating something even more daunting—an excursion into the No Spin Zone.

Bush's advisers knew that *The O'Reilly Factor* draws a huge audience in California, a state that George W. needed to win. So the stage was set—Governor Bush would sit down with your humble correspondent for thirty minutes. I don't know how he felt about it, but I was pumped. (By the way, the Gore people continued to avoid the *Factor*, as they would throughout the entire campaign.)

Although I had never met Mr. Bush before, the moment he

walked into the room he bellowed, "William, good to see you!" I immediately flashed back to the spring of 1976 when then governor Jimmy Carter got off his campaign plane at Love Field in Dallas and walked right over to a young correspondent who was working for WFAA-TV, the ABC affiliate in Big D.

"Bill, nice to finally meet you," said Governor Carter.

I was shocked. How the hell did this guy know who I was? (At the time, not all that many people knew who *he* was.) His unexpected greeting was disarming. It threw me off my game (I was very young), and Carter waltzed through the interview.

George W. Bush did not share Carter's good fortune, because I am now a grizzled veteran of the news business who has seen it all (or think I have). But Mr. Bush's greeting was disarming as well, I have to admit. He is a warm guy in public, and as we were being miked for sound, we began chatting about the campaign and his daily physical regimen. Mr. Bush seemed relaxed, but his eyes had a kind of faraway look. I believe he was going over his "script"— the points his handlers suggested he make on the *Factor*. At that time Bush was pounding "fuzzy math," "compassionate conservatism," and "reformer with results" in every interview and speech. I knew I had to blow him out of his mind-set.

The way to do that swiftly in a TV interview is to ask a question the interviewee is not expecting, one that requires him or her to think, not recite. Very few journalists these days use this technique because it can upset the subject of the interview. But this is a great technique for getting genuine responses. Viewers get so many canned answers because the interviewees know what the reporters are going to ask. Many reporters are lazy and afraid and fall back on the predictable.

Of course (he says self-servingly) the No Spin Zone rejects predictability entirely and lives to ask questions that require actual *thought*, a word anathema to most politicians in this age of spin. Therefore, after warming up George W. Bush with a few general questions, I lobbed a grenade that blasted him into the Zone.

O'REILLY: So far in this campaign what stands out in my mind regarding you is the "Jesus Christ political philosopher" remark in one of the New Hampshire debates. Everybody remembers that. [At this point Mr. Bush started to wince.] But when I heard you say that Jesus was your philosopher model, I had no problem with it. I said, "You know, that's a legitimate answer." [Mr. Bush's expression immediately went from a wince to a beam.] Certainly Jesus was a philosopher, certainly he addressed politics—render to Caesar and all that. But somebody might say, "Gee, if Governor Bush is so influenced by Jesus Christ, how can he support the death penalty so avidly, because Jesus would not have?" [Here Mr. Bush's eyes widened just a tad.]

GEORGE W. BUSH: Well, first let me say that this was not a calculated answer. It was one of those moments of time where . . . well . . . Christ just came right out of my mouth. Because Christ has influenced me, thanks to Billy Graham, who planted a seed in my heart. And it changed my life, it really did. I take great solace, I've recognized I'm humble, a little sinner. We can have a lot of issues that relate to Christianity and I, I don't want to put words in Christ's mouth. I can't justify the death penalty in terms of the New Testament. I'm going to justify it in terms of the law, and in terms of saving people's lives. I believe that the death penalty when administered surely, swiftly, and justly saves people's lives. I believe it sends a chilling signal that if you kill somebody in my state in the commission of a crime, there's going to be a consequence and you're not going to like it.

O'REILLY: So you might disagree with Jesus on this one? I don't believe he would be embracing the death penalty if he were here today. But I could be wrong.

GEORGE W. BUSH: We can both agree on this. Far be it from me to put words into the mouth of the savior.

That opening salvo forced candidate Bush to depart from his well-rehearsed script. From then on, the interview picked up speed. One of the highlights was this exchange over the conduct of Janet Reno, Bill Clinton's attorney general.

O'REILLY: Talking about corruption, Maria Hsia was just found guilty in the Buddhist Temple fund-raising scheme [involving Al Gore]. By all accounts—Charles LaBella's account, Louis Freeh's account—Ms. Reno has not pursued the campaign finance investigation very hard. If you're elected, do you investigate Attorney General Reno?

GEORGE W. BUSH: You know, I don't know. But I'll tell you what I will do and that is put in an attorney general that will uphold the law.

O'REILLY: Why wouldn't you investigate Ms. Reno?

GEORGE W. BUSH: Well, we'll see. But I don't want to make national news saying, "George Bush is going to investigate Janet Reno."

O'REILLY: All right, let's put it this way: What kind of job do you think Ms. Reno has done?

GEORGE W. BUSH: I think she's been exactly what you said. She hasn't been aggressive enough at pursuing campaign finance law violations. It's an issue, I agree.

O'REILLY: So you'd look into it?

GEORGE W. BUSH: That's how a president ought to be judged. Yes I would.

As I write, no one in the Bush administration has moved to investigate the former attorney general. She is happily retired in South Florida, giving speeches and reportedly writing a book (*The No Probe Zone?*). She continues to avoid any and all serious interview requests, and when she does show up for an appearance, she "no-comments" the questioner to death. This so-called public servant has some major nerve.

As for the death penalty, with all due respect to the president, you don't have to put words into Jesus' mouth to infer what he might have thought on the subject. Most theologians believe he considered all life sacred and, thus, would most likely oppose the death penalty. Also, since he was a victim of it, he may have a rooting interest in seeing it abolished. In the interest of fairness some other very learned spiritual people disagree with me, although the pope concurs.

For the record, 100 people were executed during Bush's six-year tenure as governor of Texas. And in mid-2001 there were 465 convicts awaiting execution in the Lone Star State.

I am against the death penalty because I feel it is too *lenient* a punishment. For example, Oklahoma City bomber Timothy McVeigh asked to be put to death and got his wish. McVeigh did not want to spend decades looking at the inside of stone walls and enjoyed going out as a martyr to his screwed-up confederates. According to some who corresponded with him, McVeigh almost relished the thought of the three different tubes of sedatives and poisons being pumped into his veins. And we accommodated him.

I've got a better idea. A punishment more appropriate—and much more terrifying—for McVeigh and others who commit crimes against humanity (this includes murder, rape, and large-quantity hard-drug dealing) would be to sentence them to life in prison in a federal penitentiary in Alaska. There they would be forced to endure hard labor, and if they refused to work, they would be quarantined in solitary confinement for twenty-three hours a day. This would effectively banish killers and rapists and condemn them to a life of harsh servitude. That is much more painful than death by injection or electricity.

There's another advantage, and we have to be honest about it. Mistakes can be made in criminal prosecutions for a variety of very human reasons. You've seen the reports about DNA or other evidence that has exonerated convicts, even some convicted of murder. It is going to happen because no system is perfect. By not executing prisoners a mistake like that can be rectified, as the convicts remain alive. (One interesting footnote: Fifty-three percent of Americans in a national poll believe there should be an execution moratorium. That poll was taken in 2001 after some law students at Northwestern University produced evidence that some Illinois death row inmates had been improperly tried.)

As you just read, President Bush argued to me that the death penalty is a deterrent, but the facts don't back him up. According to the Bureau of Justice Statistics, the murder rate in the South is higher than in any other section of the country. Yet the South accounts for 80 percent of state executions. The Northeast, on the other hand, has less than 1 percent of American executions and also has the lowest murder rate despite the population density of big cities like Philadelphia, Boston, and New York.

Why is this? Well, what many Americans fail to understand is that there are criminals who do not *care* whether they live or die. Their blighted lives mean little to them, and they are willing to risk death to achieve whatever criminal gratification they want. But are they willing to risk tremendous suffering over decades? Think about it. Ongoing hard labor in a remote location with zero amenities (this means no cable) is a horrifying prospect. Videotapes of that kind of capital punishment could be shown in every public high school in the country. You want deterrence? That's deterrence!

Okay, I think I hear the wringing of hands. (How alert am I?) Am I suggesting a gulag? You bet I am. Is it cruel and unusual punishment? Only if you believe that killers and rapists and drug kingpins have a right to live in surroundings where their friends and relatives can visit and the commissary is stocked with cigarettes and candy.

I don't believe vicious criminals should have any comforts beyond the exception of reading materials and perhaps a radio. But there are plenty of Americans who are downright sympathetic to those who commit capital crimes. Some even see poor criminals as *victims*.

Bianca Jagger is a noted figure in the anti-capital-punishment crowd in America. A poised and attractive woman from Nicaragua, Ms. Jagger achieved fame when she married Mick Jagger of the Rolling Stones in 1971. Since her divorce from the raucous rocker, Ms. Jagger has traveled all over the world preaching against capital punishment.

At age fifty-one Bianca Jagger remains a striking-looking woman. She is passionate and articulate and showed no fear when entering the No Spin Zone.

O'REILLY: I am against the death penalty but for a different reason than you are, Ms. Jagger. I don't see it as a deterrent, and a better punishment would be banishment and hard labor.

JAGGER: I'm against the death penalty in all cases because it is unfairly applied. The people who are receiving it are poor in disproportionate numbers.

O'REILLY: Statistics show that violent crimes are committed more by minorities than whites, proportionally speaking. For example, blacks make up 13 percent of the population but commit 30 percent of the violent crime. So of course you're going to have inequities in sentencing.

JAGGER: Let's talk about appropriate legal representation. Is it because minorities who are poorer than whites get worse legal representation?

O'REILLY: You know that's true. Because if you are getting something from the government for free, it is not going to be as good as when you pay for your own lawyer. They are not going to give you Johnnie Cochran for free. Come on.

JAGGER: The fact is that the poor are getting the death penalty because they have worse lawyers, not because they commit worse crimes. How many people who were innocent were executed?

O'REILLY: Ms. Jagger, your organization and others like it have not been able to come up with one person, not one, who has been proved to be innocent and executed.

JAGGER: It is believed that twenty-three people were executed that were innocent.

O'REILLY: Believed, not proved.

JAGGER: I believe we must do better research like in Illinois, where they were able to prove that thirteen people who were on death row were innocent and wrongly convicted.

O'REILLY: No, Ms. Jagger. The students at Northwestern uncovered evidence that warranted further investigations perhaps leading to new trials.

JAGGER: The application of the death penalty is unfair, racist, and biased.

O'REILLY: So what would you do with people who murder?

JAGGER: Give them life in prison without parole.

O'REILLY: But is it enough to have them sit there watching cable

TV, lifting weights, and having sex with their cellmates? I mean, that doesn't sound like a big punishment to me. Would you favor my system of banishment and hard labor?

JAGGER: I never thought about it.

So as you've seen, the unlikely duo of Bianca Jagger and President Bush has something in common: Neither one has really thought through the completely difficult but extremely important issue of capital punishment. As opposed as their beliefs are, each is espousing a locked-in position, but both opinions have disturbing loose ends.

Studies show that executions do not deter capital crimes, and the reality of America's prison system is that murderers and rapists often continue to terrorize other people within prison walls. There must be a better way to deal with the worst criminals among us. Killing them provides society with revenge but little else. Warehousing them is not punishment enough. Ms. Jagger is right when she says a poor person is far more likely to be executed than a rich person who commits the same crime. But there is no solution to that problem except to tell the poor flat out: You are up against it if you do the deed.

Both George W. Bush and Bianca Jagger believe in their hearts that they are right. Both, I believe, are wrong. Society is not obliged to kill but is obliged to dispense justice. I hope Ms. Jagger realizes that "sympathy for the devil" is sympathy wasted. And I pray the president rethinks his position and comes to embrace Jesus' scriptural philosophy that "vengeance is mine, saith the Lord."

And now that we have covered death with Mr. Bush, it is only fitting that we go on to taxes. The two things that all of us have in common.

CHAPTER ELEVEN

Your Money and Your Life

ISSUE 11: Taxes in America

THE OPPONENTS: Mario Cuomo, former
governor of New York, and David Walker, comptroller
of the United States and head of the Government
Accounting Office

O'REILLY: What about the Department of Education? It doesn't know where $450 million is. The GAO—you guys—pinpointed the missing money. Tell me about it.

WALKER: We know some of the issues. They have fundamental financial-management problems. They don't have adequate controls. They don't have adequate accountability. They lost a lot of money. There's no question about it.

O'REILLY: And you don't know where that money went, do you?

WALKER: I can't tell you where it went.

You know that I am not easily shocked. I've reported on the ground in active war zones from El Salvador to the Falkland Islands, and in chaotic situations like the collapse of the Berlin Wall and the Rodney King riots in Los Angeles.

I have interviewed people who are pure evil. People like baby killer Joel Steinberg, former SS guards at Dachau, Mafia hit men, and others. Very little surprises me.

But I am constantly amazed that millions of Americans do not see the shell game the U.S. government has been playing with our tax money. Putting it in simple terms, our tax system is beyond punitive and beyond confiscatory. In fact, it is nothing less than a program of exploitation of everyone who works hard for a living in this country.

In the last years of the Clinton administration, 26,000 very special Americans received $8.5 million in food stamps. The reason that these Americans were special is that they were dead at the time the food stamps arrived. As the Church Lady says, "Isn't that special?"

During that same period of time, the General Accounting Office estimates that more than $100 *billion* was erroneously sent to Medicare recipients.

Of course it is we the taxpayers who fund all this waste. As of January 2001, when President Bush took office, U.S. taxes were at their highest level since World War II—a time of grave national crisis and an unquestionable need for spending for national survival. But in our present time of national prosperity and peace, candidate Bush campaigned on cutting taxes across the board. But even after his election, the polls continued to show that the American people were lukewarm about such tax cuts.

I don't get it. Have you looked at your paycheck lately? Or have you just given up?

Or do you agree with the editorial writers at the *New York Times* and other well-heeled publications and the Clintonite Democrats that tax cuts only benefit the rich? That's how the spin went down: massive tax cuts for the wealthy, not much for the poor and for the blue-collar workers. Never mind that most poor Americans cannot receive a federal income tax cut for the simple reason that they *do not pay any* federal income tax because of the earned income tax credit. And never mind that the lowest tax bracket dropped the most (five percentage points). The antitax propaganda worked.

Perhaps we're just numb and don't recognize that America is a functioning "tax culture." Almost every action we take in our daily lives, from the necessary to the frivolous, activates a tax consequence. And it's not just the feds. Following the lead of the pinheads in Washington, the Siphon on the Potomac, state and local governments have slapped excises on everything from blood transfusions and children's vaccinations to hiring somebody to cut your lawn. This situation is quite simply insane. It is dragging us down personally—it is damaging the fabric of our country.

Let's be clear: If our tax dollars were being used effectively to solve social problems, to alleviate suffering and provide protection for American families, I'd shut up. If we all share in strengthening the nation by contributing monies that are honestly and fairly used, then we all benefit.

But that's not what's happening. Government waste is staggering. Incompetence, apathy, and fraud permeate D.C. like humidity in the summer. Your hard-earned money is being thrown into the incinerator and nobody in power seems to care. I am going to prove this once and for all in the next few pages—so call up Ted Kennedy and settle in.

Let's take it step by step. According to the Tax Foundation, the average American working person works three hours out of eight *each day* in order to pay his or her federal taxes. Bottom line for the typical American worker: Forty percent of your pay is being torn out of your wallet by various forms of government. Forty percent! Talk about an outrage.

In big cities like New York, Los Angeles, San Francisco, Chicago, and Boston, the cost of housing and general living expenses combined with the crushing tax burden leaves little left over for any kind of financial security. This isn't Sweden, where costs are controlled and the necessities of life are often provided free by the socialist government. This is America, where one catastrophic illness can financially ruin many families.

America is also a place where the free market dominates and we pay through the nose for anything of quality. If you want to send your kids to Harvard or Georgetown or Stanford, you better have some money in the bank or a scholarship-track child. Is it fair that only wealthy Americans can afford top-quality education? Is it fair that working Americans cannot earn enough after taxes to compete with the rich?

Not to bore you with statistics, but the government hits you for an average of 43 cents on every gallon of gasoline you buy. Each toll telephone call is taxed at 3 percent. Want to heat your house? The feds will nail you for 25 cents a gallon for heating oil. And don't think you can drink to forget your tax woes—the government takes a 58 percent duty on bottles of hard liquor.

The list goes on and on and on. Yet if you drive around New York City and other big towns, you'll see highways that people in Zambia would snicker at. John F. Kennedy International Airport looks like London after the Blitz. The "Big Dig" in Boston cost the American taxpayers billions in cost overruns (even those of us who don't live in Beantown paid, because the federal government supplemented the local funding).

And don't forget the Pentagon. The Osprey helicopter project has cost Americans more than $40 billion since 1982 and the bird is still not ready for prime time. The Osprey takes off and lands vertically and can fly like an airplane, but it has one rather large problem. It doesn't always fly right. Twice the Osprey has crashed and twenty-three marines have been killed in those incidents. Now some marine commanders refuse to let their troops fly in the Osprey because they believe it is unsafe at any angle. But do we hear outrage from any elected official in Washington? The only sound is *cha-ching*. There goes another billion of taxpayer money.

And then there are the government programs that simply don't work. The Great Society programs created by Lyndon Johnson were supposed to stamp out poverty in America. The key word here is *supposed*. The poverty rate in 2001 is pretty much the same as it was thirty-five years ago.

The massive entitlement spending did benefit some Americans along the way, but welfare was a disaster. One result: the creation of a semipermanent underclass that views government subsidies as their "right."

Because government bureaucrats refused to supervise welfare payments adequately, hundreds of billions of tax dollars went down the drain. To this day, the busiest time of the month for liquor stores and street dope dealers is the day the welfare checks arrive. Did President Johnson and his Great Society architects not know that sending checks to people without supervision might lead to the abuse of the money? Did they not understand that? Or did they not care, preferring to bask in the adulation that compassionate rhetoric inevitably brings?

And then there's the sinkhole called the Department of Education. Title One programs were set up with the noble goal of improving education for America's disadvantaged children. Twenty-five years and $125 billion later, 60 percent of poor kids in the fourth grade can barely read. For black kids the figure is 63 percent. Bush's secretary of education, Dr. Roderick Paige, is quoted as saying that Title One spending has been a total failure.

So the question is, who is keeping score? Who is watching our tax dollars, and who is making sure that federally funded programs actually work? Ready? Nobody is. With trillions in annual spending, *there is no government agency that actually watches the money!* That's right. Congress allocates the money, but there is no separate government department to oversee its use. The General Accounting Office is called in only when there is a suspicion of fraud.

This means that people who receive federal money do not have to account for it unless asked. You have trillions of federal dollars floating around basically unsupervised by anyone other than the Congresspeople who allotted the money in the first place in order to fund their campaign promises and pet projects. Do you think they want you to know that their spending is fraught with waste and fraud? The answer is no.

When things get totally out of control (like the Department of Education), the GAO swings into action. But again that agency does not routinely audit federal expenditures. So by the time the GAO gets on the case, *the money is already gone*. And the heavy odds are it is not going to be recovered.

So one more time. What we have here in America is trillions of tax dollars being spent every year and no firm system of spending accountability. The next time you hear Hillary Clinton whining about paying down the debt, just know that Mrs. Clinton and most other politicians ran up that debt by failing to establish an efficient system of preventing tax money from being wasted or stolen. They should be ashamed, but they are not. In fact, Al Gore ran on the platform of greatly expanding federal spending and conveniently forgot to address the scourge of government waste.

It is your money that is being flushed down the john, and the process is never-ending. The withholding in your paycheck is one giant river of currency that flows unimpeded to Washington, with tributary streams to your state capital, mayor's office, and county commission. This mighty Mississippi will never run dry. So let's party hardy and spend that coin.

That's what's going on and no honest person can deny it. Few politicians care about watching your tax dollars—they care about spending them. That's because most federal and state expenditures are designed to get votes. Why do you think the teachers' unions love the Democrats? Why do you think Boeing loves the Republicans? The left diverts tax dollars toward vivid visions of entitlements dancing in voters' heads; the right buys support by advocating increased spending for the military (hello, missile shield) and corporate welfare.

But the big-dollar promises are paid courtesy of the guy paving over a pothole on your local highway. And the lady grinding out memos for a demanding boss. Without access to the weekly paychecks of the vast working class, our "public servants" might actually have to pick up a shovel or learn some office skills themselves.

Shameful and dishonest, tragic and appalling—the waste of our hard-earned tax dollars is the single most scandalous part of American politics. But if we can believe the polls, few Americans care about the tax issue because it is complicated and boring and is spun to death by an avalanche of contradictory or confusing statistics and gross distortions.

In other words, this is serious grist for the No Spin Zone and its head honcho (me). I am deeply offended by the callous disregard politicians have for our money. So the Zone invited the head of the GAO to entertain the thought of a discussion.

David M. Walker is the comptroller of the United States and a man who I believe is trying his best to supervise a chaotic situation. But, as you will see, Mr. Walker's task is just about hopeless.

Here's what I said on my television program before introducing Mr. Walker: "Who is watching how our tax money is spent? Each government agency or department keeps books, and individual officers of the agencies audit all expenses. Those audits are then sent to the U.S. Treasury and to Congress. The Treasury consolidates the audits into financial 'statements'—stay with me—and sends those to the GAO."

If that sounds confusing, it is, especially when we try to get specific information, like how much did Hillary Clinton's trip to North Africa cost, where is the $5 billion the Department of Agriculture can't find, and what specifically happened to the billion dollars the Clinton administration sent to Haiti?

I then brought out David Walker, and the Zone dance began.

O'REILLY: Can you blame me for being confused about the General Accounting Office, Mr. Walker?

WALKER: I can't blame you, Bill. The fact is that millions of Americans think that we keep the books and records and look at every dime the government spends, and that's not true.

O'REILLY: We have been trying for more than a year to find out how much money Hillary Clinton, Chelsea, and their entourage spent in their two-week jaunt to North Africa. We cannot find out. Can you, Mr. Walker?

WALKER: The entity that's responsible for keeping track of that is the Office of Administration and Management in the White

House. All we know is that the lift cost—the expense of flying her around on that trip—was about $2.3 million.

O'REILLY: But you have no idea about the cost of the entire trip to the taxpayer?

WALKER: That's correct, because some of the information is not available.

O'REILLY: What? What? Wait a minute! What do you mean it's not available? That's my money Hillary was spreading around over there!

WALKER: Well, the Secret Service expense is not available for public distribution [for security reasons].

O'REILLY: Besides that, Mr. Walker, can you tell me about the other expenses?

WALKER: I can't tell you.

O'REILLY: That's not right, Mr. Walker. I'm not criticizing you, but it's not right that Hillary Clinton gets a spring break with Chelsea and her entourage and we don't know how much it cost more than two years later. Okay, what about the Department of Education? It doesn't know where $450 million is. The GAO—you guys—pinpointed the missing money. Tell me about it.

WALKER: We know some of the issues. They have fundamental financial-management problems. They don't have adequate controls. They don't have adequate accountability. They lost a lot of money. There's no question about it.

O'REILLY: And you don't know where that money went, do you?

WALKER: I can't tell you where it is.

O'REILLY: All right, let's go on to Haiti. Three billion dollars to Haiti [was sent by the Clinton administration]. One billion of that nobody seems to be able to account for. Do you know where it is?

WALKER: I don't know where it is, but let me clarify one thing. Each major department and agency has an inspector general whose job it is to fight waste, fraud, abuse, and mismanagement in their own department. Congress is responsible for doing the oversight. If Congress doesn't call us in, we don't know anything.

O'REILLY: I understand that, but here's the deal. We have massive taxation in this country. Forty cents out of every dollar a worker earns is taken by the system. I just gave you three examples—and I could give you thirty more—of money that is unaccounted for. Again, I'm not blaming you, Mr. Walker, but don't tell me that the American public should not know how much Hillary Clinton is spending, shouldn't know where a billion dollars to Haiti went, and shouldn't know about gross waste in various departments, because we should.

WALKER: Bill, I understand your point. One of the things we need, quite frankly, is a modern, integrated, financial-management system for the entire government. Brazil has one, but we don't have one in the United States.

O'REILLY: You know, Mr. Walker, that is one of the most truthful things any government employee has ever said on this program. We need a central authority that can monitor all taxpayer expenditures, because what we have now is chaotic and the bandits can get away with all kinds of stuff.

In my opinion, David Walker is an honest man. And, to be fair, the GAO under his guidance did save us taxpayers about $23 billion in the year 2000 by getting refunds for overpayments and similar actions. But that is just a small percentage of the enormous waste that is built into all levels of government.

Of course the politicians know the system is corrupt and chaotic, but to them this is a *good* thing. It is far easier to reward supporters with spending projects that are basically unsupervised. Campaigning for office is really about promising things. The more unsupervised money there is, the more promises that can be fulfilled and the more fun that can be had by the lucky "in" crowd.

The Clintons, all-time champions of making promises, took advantage of the tax money situation to an extent never before seen in America. Pursuing Hillary Clinton's 1998 junket to North Africa, my staff and I followed the spending trail right to Hillary's doorstep. But then we were stopped cold. You see, according to a federal law called the Presidential Records Act, occupants of the White House do not have to turn over any documents, including expenses, for five years after they leave Pennsylvania Avenue. What a scam! Hillary Clinton's office told my investigators to "fly off." They laughed in our faces as they quoted the Records Act.

But here is what I was able to ascertain with the help of GAO reports and analysis by the National Taxpayers Union. In the eight years they spent in the White House, Mr. and Mrs. Clinton spent close to—take a breath—$525 million of taxpayer money for their travels. This is by far the most money ever spent by a president and First Lady in that area. And what do we the people get for all that travel? Well, you can make that call.

And what did Bill Clinton get? In his first five months out of office he visited nearly two dozen countries and picked up approximately $5 million in speaking fees. The relationships he made abroad while president have certainly paid off.

Unfortunately, the Clintons are far from being the only ones who've made careers and names for themselves by trumpeting their noble intentions while at the same time carefully skirting the issue of accountability. The soaring rhetoric of people like Ronald Reagan and Mario Cuomo often emphasized their great vision for the USA and their sympathetic understanding of the downtrodden. But much of the talk turned out to be very, very expensive for you and me.

Once again, this is not about compassion or helping Americans who need help. Most of us support that noble goal. But without financial accountability and rigid supervision, compassionate programs hurt more Americans (working-class taxpayers) than they help (financially strapped citizens). Talk is cheap. Giant entitlement programs like free health insurance and prescription drugs are incredibly expensive. But those who champion massive entitlements feel very comfortable on the high moral ground.

Take, for example, former New York governor Mario Cuomo's keynote address to the 1984 Democratic Convention. Fine writing delivered well by one of the most effective orators of our time, Cuomo's speech detailing his view of America's responsibility to our poorest citizens was a smash hit and put him into presidential contention. The speech not only affected the national debate on domestic policy; it also led to millions of dollars of speaking fees for Mario Cuomo. In 1992, in order to calm left-leaning Democrats who thought nominee Bill Clinton might be too much of a centrist, Governor Cuomo was asked to deliver Clinton's nominating speech at the party convention in New York City.

Mario Cuomo served as New York governor from 1983 to 1994. During the Reagan boom years, he was one of the biggest spenders in state history, increasing New York's expenditures by a whopping 10 percent a year. In order to fund his programs, Cuomo had to raise taxes and did so with a vengeance. By the early nineties the governor was hiking up taxes by a billion or more *each year*. One disastrous result was a business exodus from New York State that cost the region more than a half million jobs. And on his watch, despite the flood of new programs and agencies, rates of welfare dependence, crime, and drug addiction soared. Cuomo's approval rating plummeted, and in 1994 he was defeated by little-known state legislator George Pataki. Even in New York, one of the most liberal places in the country, voters wanted tax relief.

Still, Mario Cuomo remains unrepentant about his tax-and-spend philosophy. Since he continues to be a Democratic icon and a smart guy, I very much wanted to get him into the Zone.

But the former governor resisted, even though his son Chris was a correspondent for the Fox News Channel that carries *The O'Reilly Factor*. Finally, when I happened to see the elder Cuomo in Rockefeller Center one day, I approached him and blurted out, "Hey, Governor, are you avoiding me? My mother says you are."

Mario Cuomo laughed and shook his head. We talked a bit and he agreed to come on my program. A few weeks later he kept his word, even though he knew the conversation would be tough, because I believe taxes are out of control.

O'REILLY: I want a tax cut.

CUOMO: I'm sure you want it.

O'REILLY: Let's help the working guy. Let's do away with the payroll tax [for Social Security] and give everybody who works an immediate 12 percent raise.

CUOMO: I have a deal for you. We should say to President Bush, "We saw you with your pictures of middle-class workers and poor workers, saying these people would get tax cuts. We love the pictures. We notice you didn't take any pictures with millionaires. We'll give you the tax cuts right now for the poor and middle class and argue about the rest later." What would you say to that, Bill?

O'REILLY: I would say that Mr. Bush doesn't believe, as you do, in income redistribution. He wants an across-the-board cut.

CUOMO: No, no, you're wrong. But, Bill, I know this [my opinion of taxes] is good for your popularity ratings. What is the space program? What is the defense budget? These are redistributions of wealth.

O'REILLY: Wait a minute. That's not redistribution.

CUOMO: Of course it is. You took my wealth and you redistributed it to purposes I didn't want.

O'REILLY: You didn't want a defense budget?

CUOMO: Not the size of it. Not the waste that it is. Not this missile defense shield.

O'REILLY: I agree with you on the waste, but not on the redistribution.

CUOMO: No, it is redistribution when I take money from you and spend it on something else.

O'REILLY: No, give it to *somebody* else, not spend it on something. For thirty years you guys in the Democratic Party have been driving entitlements for the poor, and the poverty rate hasn't changed. One more question. I'm for a national sales tax in place of the payroll tax. Would you favor that?

CUOMO: Not instead of a progressive tax which would take you who makes millions of dollars—you deserve it—and say, now you only want to pay the same tax as me and I'm homeless?

O'REILLY: Come on, Governor. I will buy far more and pay far more in taxes for doing so.

CUOMO: That's nice if you're rich. It's not nice if you are middle class or poor. And that's why we don't have it, because there are more working-class people than O'Reillys.

O'REILLY: Governor, I'm still carrying the load by buying an expensive car and home. I'm paying far more in taxes than someone who's living modestly.

CUOMO: Of course. If you can afford the big car, you don't care. But what about people who can't afford things?

O'REILLY: Going to a national sales tax just gave them a 12 percent raise as the payroll tax is abolished. I'll give you the last word.

CUOMO: The truth is that you can make the weaker part of this country much stronger without making the stronger part weaker by giving people better education, better health care, better protection at their work site, and paying more attention to the middle class and poor. People see that.

What a wrap-up! Concise, effective, right on the dot for people who support his point of view. The governor is still a master of rhetoric—but I firmly believe that he is wrong.

He and many other liberal Americans love so-called progressive taxation; in other words, they want to take money from the wealthy and give it to Americans who "need" it more. As I stated, my national sales tax plan would pay for sharply focused entitlements to the less fortunate by taxing people on what they *spend* rather than on what they *earn*. If you work hard, then you'd have far more control over your take-home pay. And poor Americans would keep every dime they make because the earned income tax credit means they already pay no federal income tax; in addition, my plan would eliminate the payroll tax everybody is paying now.

But that is not enough for Governor Cuomo and many others. They want the power to take money from the wealthy. The rich already pay the vast majority of federal income tax, as President Clinton raised the top tax bracket to 39.9 percent. President Bush has scaled it back to 36 percent, but in big tax states like New York a top-wage earner brushes up against a 50 percent levy and that's not counting all the add-ons (sales tax, property tax, etc.). I do not weep for the Donald Trumps of the world, but I do ask this fundamental question: Was America set up to take money from one citizen and give it to another?

During the depression of the 1930s, this philosophy was embraced by President Franklin Delano Roosevelt, who said, "Our revenue laws have operated in many ways to the unfair advantage of the few, and they have done little to prevent an unjust concentration of wealth and economic power."

Roosevelt was right and wrong. All Americans should pay their fair share, and some fat cats were avoiding taxes in the Roaring Twenties. The need for financial supervision at the federal level was obvious, and Roosevelt kicked it in, becoming a champion of the working class in the process. And even today some wealthy Americans continue to exploit our capitalist system (hello to the Clinton-pardoned Marc Rich).

But no system is perfect and the United States is not Sweden. America was set up so that individuals could prosper and take it to the capitalistic limit. If that system is no longer valid, we should hold a national debate and vote on it. But to federally impose quasi-socialism goes against our heritage and has been proved to be a failure. Time and time again, the entitlement culture championed by people like Mario Cuomo has failed, and trillions of tax dollars have been wasted on programs that *sounded* good.

If I believed "progressive" taxation led to lessening of social problems, I would be Governor Cuomo's best ideological friend. But I deal in facts, not Land of Oz fantasies. Hard work and discipline lead to economic success. Government handouts and unsupervised policies of pity only rob people of incentive. If tax money continues to be wasted, it becomes morally wrong for our government to confiscate huge percentages of income and property from Americans, even if they are wealthy. Right now our national slogan is "The more you make, the more we take. And we're not even going to watch how we spend it."

Welfare has failed. Public housing is a shambles. Public education is a mess. The poverty rate remains unchanged. And yet the big government beat goes on.

In 1766 Benjamin Franklin warned the British Parliament that if the stamp tax wasn't repealed, the colonies might well revolt. Today our tax situation is revolting (sorry), but too many of us remain passive in the face of it. The road to hell is paved with good intentions—and you know what? Those intentions are being paid for big-time by all working Americans. It is enough to test even the strongest person's sobriety. Which brings us to another vexing problem: drugs.

CHAPTER TWELVE

I Want to Take You Higher

ISSUE 12: America's drug culture

THE OPPONENTS: John McCain, senator from Arizona; Barry McCaffrey, former drug czar; and Ted Demme, Hollywood director

DEMME: [This drug dealer] had come from a family where he had seen his father work his entire life harder than he should have, with nothing to show for it. And he didn't have any good role models around to show him what a good day's pay would earn and how to earn a proper living. You have to understand these guys.

O'REILLY: My father worked hard his whole life and he didn't have a lot to show for it.

DEMME: Well, mine did too.

O'REILLY: And we don't sell drugs, do we?

The United States government does not want to win the war on drugs. I firmly believe this, based upon my years of reporting and interviewing those involved. Despite expenditures north of $30 billion a year fighting illegal narcotics, there is more dope on the streets of America than ever before, and, according to the Drug Enforcement Agency, the drugs get purer and more addictive every year.

So what's the deal?

Well, the truth is that the powers-that-be simply do not have the courage to take the difficult and controversial steps necessary to control the lucrative narcotics business. Big business always frightens politicians and this is very big business.

Here's a glimpse of how big:

- There are in excess of 10 million "heavy drug users" in the United States.

- Approximately 70 percent of street crime is drug related.

- Approximately 70 percent of all child abuse is committed by substance abusers (this includes those who abuse alcohol).

- There are more than 1 million DUI arrests annually in the United States.

With statistics like that, even someone high on ecstasy or crank could figure it out: Intoxication is a horrendous problem in America.

Now for a dose of reality. No government is ever going to stop all its citizens from intoxicating themselves. Ever. There have always been and will always be substance abusers. We must start there.

As far as I'm concerned, if the abuser keeps it inside, I don't care. You want to stay stoned all day long, fine—as long as you don't hurt your children (although just that scenario hurts them) or ask me to chip in for your welfare check. Get stoned—but stay off the streets.

But if you intrude on my freedom while intoxicated, then I have a big problem with you, and the government has a responsibility to side with me. I want to be protected from you. I don't want you in my face or around my family. And I have a right under equal protection of the law to demand that. I don't want you providing a terrible example for my children. I don't want you using my tax money to get high. And I don't want you behind the wheel of any vehicle.

Unfortunately, the government at this point is not taking my rights seriously. The authorities are allowing drug markets to exist, and some of them are right out in the open. Those are usually in the poor neighborhoods, and that is a subtle form of racism if there ever was one. And rather than treat the minority of dope-heads who actually want to quit the habit, law enforcement often allows drug offenders to leave custody without any requirement for follow-up drug testing.

And that's just the beginning of our government's irresponsible and socially dangerous behavior. The feds simply will not properly patrol the border with Mexico for fear of "offending" that country. And severe penalties are often not imposed on street dope pushers. These life-destroying criminals, considered pariahs in a saner era, are now even lionized in some movies, recordings, and TV shows.

There are three basic strategies needed to control America's drug problem. First, impose coerced drug rehab on all criminals who are arrested and test positive for narcotics. Second, use the U.S. military to assist the Border Patrol from Brownsville, Texas, to Imperial Beach, California, and use the Navy to assist the Coast Guard. And third, sentence major and persistent drug sellers to banishment in faraway federal penitentiaries.

I have discussed the coerced drug-rehabilitation strategy in detail in my book *The O'Reilly Factor*. Rather than repeat myself, I'll just explain that the basic idea is to empower authorities to keep drug-involved criminals off the streets for months and sometimes years in therapeutic drug prisons. The aim is to change their behavior drastically. They would be provided with psychological help as well as life-skill training. Upon release from the facility, the person would be drug-tested every few days. Anyone who tests dirty goes back inside. This program has impressively reduced recidivism in Alabama. It works.

My second strategy would cut the drug flow across the southern border in half within months. Using high-tech surveillance gear, our military could interdict not only drugs but also other types of contraband and stem the flow of illegal immigrants at the same time. Remember, the military's mandate is "to protect the borders" of our country. President Bush the elder declared drug importation a national security problem and he was right. There is no reason on this earth why the highly trained and effective U.S. military is not being used to prevent the flow of drugs into the country. When you have a national security problem, and the drug problem is certainly one, deal with it.

My third strategy is based upon one simple fact: Drug dealers are scum. So far as they're concerned, I've got the same question I asked in chapter one about the NAMBLA degenerates: Where's the outrage? Where is public opinion? Why are these people not shunned for being the corrupters they are? Like the ACLU on NAMBLA, we are accepting the unacceptable if a person selling narcotics does not anger us. Back in the 1960s my father told me that anyone who dealt dope was a parasite, a person beneath contempt. I always remembered that. How many children are being told that today, especially in the ghetto neighborhoods? What do kids think when they encounter the sleazy dealer?

This story may provide a sad clue: As a correspondent for ABC News in 1988, I did a story about drug trafficking in South-Central Los Angeles. I went into a housing project and began interviewing people. A large crowd gathered and I asked, "Is there anyone here who is morally opposed to drug dealing?" No one raised his or her hand. They might have been frightened, but after an initial short silence I heard all kinds of excuses. "The dealers give us money." "The white man controls the drug trade." "There's nothing wrong with getting high."

No one stepped forward and said, "Man, these pushers are ruining the weakest among us, including children. They sell poison. They are parasites."

Until Americans of every stripe step up and say just that—and demand that the police sweep drug dealers off the streets—the dope war will not be won. Until public pressure forces our apathetic and frightened politicians to get really tough on those who sell narcotics, Americans will continue to die with needles in their arms, prostitute themselves, infect each other with the AIDS virus, and steal anything they can. How much heartache has to pass through the nation before society reacts? Are you going to wait until it's your child with the drug problem?

As for the media, their delayed reaction and their lack of responsibility have been, generally speaking, disgraceful. If the stars aren't flaunting their own personal drug use (Eminem, Cheech and Chong), they are participating in projects that glorify drugs and alcohol (and cigarettes for that matter). Movies have made brilliant use of charismatic stars and flashy cinematography to make the drug world look lucrative and normal. Business as usual, babes ahoy.

One such project is the movie *Blow*, starring Johnny Depp and Penelope Cruz, two attractive actors who directly appeal to young people. The film is based on the life of convicted cocaine dealer George Jung, who is currently serving twenty years in prison.

Before the system finally caught up with Jung, he smuggled drugs for more than twenty years, supplying thousands of tons of cocaine to millions of Americans. He accumulated millions of dollars that he spent on himself. Women threw themselves at him. The Jung party was constant and unrelenting and the movie documents all of it.

What the film does not address is that many people became hooked from using Jung's stuff. How many people died or became crack whores or gave birth to addicted children because George Jung was in business? Hollywood was not interested in that tale.

The director of *Blow*, Ted Demme, is an accomplished professional. But he does not see George Jung the same way that I see him. So the stage was set as Demme blew into the No Spin Zone.

O'REILLY: I think dealing hard drugs like cocaine is a crime against humanity. And I would give guys like George Jung more than twenty years in prison.

DEMME: I mean, look, George Jung is fifty-eight years old. And this guy is an ex–drug addict and I think these guys need rehab more than hard time.

O'REILLY: He's selling drugs for what—twenty-five years?

DEMME: Since 1968 probably.

O'REILLY: He makes millions, right? He gets to hang around with ladies like Penelope Cruz. He lives a life that hardworking Americans could never live. Luxury. Then he gets caught. And you're telling me, Mr. Demme, that he shouldn't be doing twenty years?

DEMME: I think the crime he was busted for didn't merit twenty years. He's not a murderer. George had come from a family where he had seen his father work his entire life harder than he should have, with nothing to show for it. And he didn't have any good role models around to show him what a good day's pay would earn and how to earn a proper living. You have to understand these guys.

O'REILLY: My father worked hard his whole life and he didn't have a lot to show for it.

DEMME: Well, mine did too.

O'REILLY: And we don't sell drugs, do we?

DEMME: He wasn't selling it. He was bringing it into this country.

O'REILLY: That's selling it, Mr. Demme.

DEMME: So he should equal a murderer?

O'REILLY: He's worse than a murderer. This guy deals for twenty-five years in weight cocaine. Untold thousands of people use this drug and some of them destroy their lives.

DEMME: No one forced them to use it. That's their own fault. The person who snorts it is responsible.

O'REILLY: If nobody sold drugs, Mr. Demme, there wouldn't be any drug addicts. And I have a problem with you too. You put together a movie that a lot of people are going to see. You've got Johnny Depp playing this Jung guy. And you yourself don't believe Jung should pay society for what he did for twenty-five years, and I'm appalled by that stance. I don't believe in capital punishment, but if I did, this guy should be dead. I've got a problem with the message you're sending.

DEMME: Bill, you're naive. Putting people in jail for life is not going to stop drug dealing. It won't stop the problem. You're in denial as much as the rest of the country is about our drug problem. The problem isn't with the people who are selling it—it's that there's no rehab, man.

Ted Demme is a powerful filmmaker, but his permissive attitude on drug dealers hurts this country. There are plenty of poor kids who would trade twenty years of living large for twenty years in prison, especially if the Ted Demmes of the world will pity them. Many critics said the message of *Blow* was ambiguous. Let me tell you it was not. Johnny Depp had a great time dealing drugs—too bad he got caught.

✳

Short of mass murder, the American media almost never condemn any antisocial activity, because there is always an excuse for the behavior. George Jung didn't have any "positive role models." Come on, this is garbage. Disgraceful people like Jung should be banished for decades if not for life. They should be forced to endure hard labor in prison. In short, they should be harshly punished for inflicting so much damage upon this country. Anything short of that is irresponsible and terribly misguided.

But the powers-that-be, the people who are supposed to counter the Ted Demmes of the world, are often woefully lacking in the kind of analytical and tough-minded thinking that would make an impression on the future George Jungs of the world. One of those persons is General Barry McCaffrey, who served for five years as President Clinton's "drug czar."

General McCaffrey is a West Point graduate who served America honorably in Vietnam. He was a controversial commander in the Gulf War, as a few of his men accused him of ordering the destruction of defenseless, fleeing Iraqis. Be that as it may, the general's most important job was to direct the United States' attack on the drug trade. But, in my opinion, the general had no effective strategy and no will to win.

My interview with him came shortly after he became the director of White House Drug Policy in 1996. At that time the No Spin Zone was not widely known, and the general was not pleased he had walked into an ambush . . .

O'REILLY: Do you have any plan at all to turn this drug thing around?

MCCAFFREY: We have a national strategy in front of the American people. It's systemic. It says, "Let's stay engaged for ten years and let's work on drug prevention and drug treatment."

O'REILLY: Well, that strategy hasn't worked in the past. I mean, we had "just say no" with Nancy Reagan. We still have plenty of drug addicts.

MCCAFFREY: The real problem is that American youngsters are doing drugs again. Since 1990 we've seen a steady erosion in their commitment to disapprove drug use.

O'REILLY: Let me stop you there. I disagree with you. Seventy percent of all street crime is caused by drug-involved people. Seventy percent of all child abuse is caused by substance abusers. Most of the AIDS cases right now are being spread by intravenous drug users. These are grim stats.

MCCAFFREY: It is clear that drug use is a grim specter. It costs America $67 billion a year in various costs. But if we get serious about the issue, we can make a difference.

O'REILLY: But you can't stop drugs from coming into the United States.

MCCAFFREY: I agree.

O'REILLY: So what are you going to do?

MCCAFFREY: You have to treat the root cause. At the end of the day you understand that a holistic approach is likely to be helpful.

With all due respect to the general, he was clueless. And five years later I think that is fully apparent. The Clinton administration did absolutely nothing to improve the drug problem in this country despite a massive amount of antidrug spending.

Will President Bush's policies be any more effective? Not likely unless he diverts federal drug funding into state-coerced rehab programs, and orders the military to police the porous southern border.

Realistically, I don't believe he will do it. The strategy is too controversial, as my viewers remind me every time I bring the subject up on the *Factor*. Also, there is not enough voter support, as many people simply don't understand the seriousness of the border situation. Finally, the action could tee off some Mexican Americans as well as the Mexican government, causing all kinds of panicked headlines for Mr. Bush. Papers like the *New York Times* would go wild conjuring up editorial images of a police state. The president's enemies in Congress would yell long and loud about misuse of power and the poor aliens and on and on.

So don't look for any bold solutions in the drug fight anytime soon. Only a leader fully committed to taking risks could dent the drug traffic, and we don't have that kind of leader in this country right now. Tomorrow, Mr. Bush could order an aggressive anti-drug campaign, damning the torpedoes and going full speed ahead. It would be a gutsy but potentially damaging move politically. And political expediency usually rules.

Not too many Americans remember, but two years ago the House of Representatives did pass a resolution that would have put the military on the border, only to see the bill die in the Senate. And one of the senators who remains opposed to the military strategy is John McCain of Arizona.

This is somewhat puzzling to me. Arizona has three hundred miles of border with Mexico, and close to 1 million people are arrested in the border area each year. That's the number *caught*—no one knows how many illegal immigrants and drug-carrying thugs are sneaking through undetected. You'd think a senator from a state plagued with these severe problems would be pleading for federal help.

And Arizona is not a wealthy state. In fact, the border problems are crippling it financially, as an estimated $150 million a year, or almost 10 percent of the state's budget, is spent trying to control the border. That money, of course, could be used to combat other social problems. For example, Arizona has the highest high school dropout rate in the country, and its educational system is in disarray.

I can't agree with Senator McCain's position, but I like him. I'm not exactly sure why (he and his campaign people were tough to deal with during the presidential primaries). But I admire his passion and his anti-establishment edge. Besides, after entering the Zone a number of times in recent years, he provided me with a slyly funny blurb for my previous book: "I just returned from a trip to Vietnam and one of the reasons I went was to prepare myself for being back on *The O'Reilly Factor* because Bill O'Reilly uses some of their old interrogation techniques."

I loved that blurb. But when I faced Senator McCain on the border issue, I brought every technique I knew to bear in order to stimulate the debate.

O'REILLY: Do you favor, Senator, putting troops on the U.S. border?

MCCAIN: I do not favor using troops because they're not trained for it. They don't have the qualifications necessary. I strongly favor us using all the technical equipment our military has, including satellites and aircraft. But our military is not trained to do the groundwork.

O'REILLY: Wait a minute, Senator. Our military is guarding the border of Korea and Bosnia right now. Surely we can train them to back up the Border Patrol and discourage illegal crossings?

MCCAIN: Our military is guarding against invasion. Our Border Patrol is the agency that can deal with this. We also have to do a lot more drug enforcement.

O'REILLY: But that hasn't worked. For twenty years it hasn't worked.

MCCAIN: The long-term answer is a healthy Mexican economy. Many of us are very encouraged by the election of Vicente Fox. We have great confidence in him.

O'REILLY: I'm not going to let you off the hook, Senator. You say that the armed forces are not trained to patrol the border, and my contention is that the men and women in the armed forces are intelligent enough to take on this assignment. It's you guys in Washington that don't have the will—and I don't know why—to solve this problem.

MCCAIN: We are a multicultural state and we're very proud of our heritage. We want to do everything possible to enforce our borders. That's our obligation to do that.

O'REILLY: Senator, Arizona's jails are overflowing. You have a million arrests on the border. Don't you have to put the American people ahead of the Mexican people?

McCAIN: Well, Bill, there are many Hispanic citizens of the state of Arizona who are proud of their culture and I'm not sure they would agree with you.

O'REILLY: So what are you going to do, then? Do you have anything new on the table to stop the drugs and the aliens?

McCAIN: Yes, we have. We have dramatically increased funding for the border. We'll continue to use military hardware but, again, the real solution to the problem is a healthy Mexican economy. We're the only nation in the world with an advanced economy that has a nation on its border that has the economy the Mexicans do, and all of this is complicated by the flow of drugs as well. Finally, I believe President Bush is well equipped and knowledgeable about this issue and has it as one of his highest priorities.

O'REILLY: Senator, always a pleasure to debate with you.

Do you agree with Senator McCain? I mean, do you really believe more spending is going to solve the border problem? Does anyone believe that? And as for making drug smuggling and border jumping less attractive by strengthening the huge, chaotic Mexican economy, that's a great idea. But do you see that happening anytime this century?

So once again we have the customary Washington answer, even from the so-called maverick senator: Pour even more money into a complicated situation and hope for an economic miracle south of the border. That's the Beltway mentality in spades. When will they ever learn? Never, that's when.

What explains this nonsense? The clue comes in Senator McCain's comments about ethnic sensitivities. The conventional wisdom in Washington runs something like this: Hispanic Americans would be insulted by the installation of troops on the border, and the Mexican politicos would go *loco en la cabeza*. Possibly, but I wonder if anyone has taken the time to ask Hispanic parents how they feel about drugs streaming across the border toward the playgrounds of their children. I bet they don't believe that multiculturalism is a reason to ignore the 22 pounds of heroin, 4,780 pounds of cocaine, and 175,000 pounds of marijuana seized at the Arizona border in 2000. I don't believe anyone thinks "ethnic pride" has anything to do with the fact that Arizona has to spend more money each year on substance abuse than on Medicaid. So what about that, Washington?

This particular interview with John McCain took place in May 2001. A day later fourteen Mexican men and teenage boys were found dead from exposure and thirst in the brutal "Devil's Path," a searing, desolate stretch of land east of Yuma in the Arizona desert. Their bodies were so dehydrated that one official described them as "mummified." They succumbed in 115-degree heat some fifty miles from the nearest road. This horror was not unprecedented. From September 30, 1999, through September 30, 2000, the bodies of 106 illegals were found near the Arizona border.

I don't believe such catastrophes would occur if the U.S. military had been patrolling there with state-of-the-art surveillance equipment. In fact, hundreds, perhaps thousands, of Mexican lives would be saved each year. In addition, the USA would be far more protected from the accelerating invasion—and that's what it is—of undocumented aliens and lethal drugs. Someone needs to remind our leaders that we have a Constitution and that it requires, among other things, that the federal government protect the states from invasion. You might tell your representatives to look it up: article IV, section 4. I read those words to refute Senator McCain, who has said publicly that putting the military on the border would be "a slippery slope of dubious constitutionality."

I stand with Dave Stoddard, formerly Border Patrol supervisor in Arizona and a twenty-seven-year veteran of the agency. Mr. Stoddard entered the Zone and made the following points:

1. The United States military is the best-equipped, best-trained, and most technologically advanced such force in the world.

2. It was his experience that the mere presence of the U.S. military on the border deters illegal aliens as well as narcotics trafficking.

3. He would put the military on the border, regain control, and deploy their numbers in strength from Brownsville, Texas, to San Diego.

Sometimes it makes sense to listen to the experts.

But I don't hear many other media voices demanding action on this problem or many of the other complicated situations we as Americans are facing. During eight years of Clintonism, the elite media, most notably the network TV news divisions, have been very wary of making any waves. They rarely investigated governmental wrongdoing, until a scandal got so big they were forced to pay attention. And Bill Clinton himself was given almost a complete pass.

But why? I won't try to tell you. I'll leave that to CBS anchorman Dan Rather, who is next up in the No Spin Zone. It was an experience we'll both remember.

CHAPTER THIRTEEN

Rather Telling

ISSUE 13: The failure of network TV news to investigate the powerful

THE OPPONENT: Dan Rather, CBS News anchorman

O'REILLY: My contention is this: that the powerful in this country protect each other. So let me ask you flat out: Do you think President Clinton is an honest man?

RATHER: Yes, I think he's an honest man.

O'REILLY: Even when he lied to the nation and to Jim Lehrer's face about the Lewinsky business?

RATHER: Who among us has not lied about something?

O'REILLY: Well, I haven't lied to anyone's face on national television.

Wow. We'll continue with that infamous Zone moment in a couple of pages, but first a little background.

We go back, Dan Rather and I . . . way back.

In 1981 I was promoted from reporter for WCBS-TV, the CBS network's flagship station in New York City, to CBS News correspondent. That leap into the national news scene is the dream of many local reporters. Dan Rather had just recently replaced Walter Cronkite, the nation's most trusted man according to the polls, as anchor for *CBS Evening News*. Rather was already famous in his own right for taking on Richard Nixon and for his aggressive, authoritative reporting all over the world. He was making it clear that he wanted to mold his news team in his relatively youthful, fearless image.

That sounded like the right fit to me. I was already known in the TV industry as a take-no-prisoners reporter. I had recently won an Emmy for investigating corruption in the New York City marshal's office, and my "no spin" approach was rapidly developing. I thought my future with the "new look" CBS News operation was going to be bright.

Saner people who knew my brash personality suspected otherwise. Some veteran newspeople warned me not to take the CBS job because, as they politely expressed it, I was not a "team player." And that was true. I was and still am a journalistic gunslinger. I look the story in the eye and shoot it down. I don't need four other people telling me what I am looking at.

Although I was too simple to realize it at the time, that kind of attitude would make many CBS News veterans dislike me right off the bat. More than a few would take absolute delight in seeing me fail. Some older people who liked me knew this, but I shrugged off their advice, only seeing the glamour of reporting for the nation's premier television news operation. I should have heeded the warnings, but as usual I swaggered in there thinking I was going to conquer the situation.

Let me elaborate a bit further on this "team player" business, since it is currently in vogue, especially in the corporate world of TV news. Good journalism is best done by a person who is honest, accurate, and observant. From the beginning of my career in Scranton, Pennsylvania, I have always written my own scripts, asked my own questions, and evaluated the validity of the answers. I find it unnecessary to have somebody else back in the broadcast center, a person who was not present at the scene of the story, rewrite my report or give me a "point of view."

Perhaps I'm conceited (I know you're shocked), but that's the way I feel about it. Why hire me to report unless you trust my reporting? I proved myself early on by rising quickly through the ranks and winning a bunch of reporting awards. In my twenty-seven years as a journalist I have never had to retract a story and I have never lost a lawsuit. I simply don't believe in reporting by "committee."

But CBS News did. The culture there dictated that new young correspondents were to do what they were told to do, say what they were told to say. And that was that: Just shut up and do it. Do you sense a collision coming between the corporation and your humble correspondent? It didn't take long.

✳

A few weeks after taking the CBS job I was flown to El Salvador to report on the war going on there at the time. I drew an assignment that sent me to the Morazán province in the mountainous northeastern part of that beautiful country. This was "Indian country," a place where the communist guerrillas *("los muchachos")* operated with impunity. It was a dangerous place, and my crew—driver, producer, and cameraman—was not thrilled to be going there.

It took us a full day to drive to Morazán from San Salvador, the capital city, because all the bridges had been blown up and we had to ford the rivers in our van. This was slow going, making us easy targets. Our only protection was a message painted in black letters over and over again on the sides of the van: *Periodistas—no dispare* (Journalists—don't shoot). None of us had much confidence that the message would be heeded.

After about eight hours on the "road" we rolled into the small town of San Francisco Gotera, the last village in the province held by the U.S.-backed-government troops. The soldiers were housed in an old-style fort complete with wooden walls. As we drove through the gates, we saw three men hanging from hooks by their tied wrists. They were being whipped. We thought they were cap-tured guerrillas.

We were wrong. It turned out that they were Salvadoran sol-diers who had fallen asleep on guard duty the night before. The captain in charge of the garrison cheerfully told me that he would have shot the men except they were under age sixteen. But the next time they did not fulfill the assignment, he would shoot them pronto. Nobody doubted his word.

El capitán also gave us the local war news. The *"muchachos"* had wiped out a small village called Meanguera a few miles to the south because its mayor was deemed friendly to the government. The atrocity had not been confirmed, though, because nobody in his right mind would go into the guerrilla-controlled area.

When I told the captain that my assignment was to check the story out, he rolled his eyes, smiled, and said, *"Vaya con Dios"* (Go with God).

God was good, and after traversing the worst road I have ever seen, we arrived in Meanguera without incident a few hours later. The place was leveled to the ground and fires were still smoldering. But even though the carnage was obviously recent, we saw no one live or dead. There was absolutely nobody around who could tell us what happened. I quickly did a stand-up amid the rubble and we got the hell out of there.

As we were making our way back to the safety of the fort, a group of heavily armed men suddenly appeared in the road ahead of us and waved for us to stop. This is one of the worst things that can happen in any out-of-control war zone. Slowly, and I mean slowly, we got out of the van with our hands up. The leader of the group, a teenager, had a bullet belt crisscrossing his chest. All the teens were wearing bandanas. Who the hell were these guys?

After eyeing us for about two minutes, the leader stepped forward and identified himself as a sergeant in the Salvadoran Army. It turned out that he and his boys were government soldiers on a reconnaissance patrol. I quickly mentioned the captain's name and that we had been up to Meanguera. They all had a big laugh over that, saying we had *cojones*. Within a few minutes we were back on the wretched but welcomed road to San Salvador.

The next day I filed my report. I explained that while a scorched-earth policy was clearly in effect in remote villages—the evidence was right there on tape—it was impossible to say just who was doing the scorching. Could be the *muchachos*, could be the government. The ninety-second package contained great video and a fairly impressive "on the scene in a very bad place" stand-up by yours truly. I was looking forward to seeing Dan Rather introduce your humble but now "macho" correspondent on *CBS Evening News*.

It never happened. When I called New York to find out the status of my story, the foreign editor said he never received it and had no idea where it was. But, he promised, he would look for it. A few days later the guy called me and said he hadn't found the El

Salvador report but, oh, by the way, "We are sending you to Argentina."

✳

In 1982 the Falkland Islands war between Great Britain and Argentina was making worldwide headlines and CBS had a huge presence in Buenos Aires, the Argentine capital. I arrived in that vast city early in the morning after an overnight flight from Miami, as per company instructions. I was told there would be a CBS driver to meet me and guide me quickly through customs. Guess what? Nobody showed up.

I was beginning to see a pattern. More than a little teed off, I made my way finally to the Buenos Aires Sheraton Hotel, where CBS News had set up offices. I got straight to the point with the bureau chief: Why had I been stranded at the airport? He crisply replied that he had more important things to worry about, and one more thing—he had no idea I was even coming! (He also had no idea who I was—me being new and all.)

Things continued downhill. What happened to me in Argentina is told in meticulous detail in my novel *Those Who Trespass*. The short version is this: All hell broke loose in Buenos Aires when the Argentines surrendered to the British. Thousands of Argentines took to the streets screaming for the head of President General Leopoldo Galtieri. Said mob stormed the Presidential Palace, the Casa Rosada, and were met by the army, which quickly opened fire. A major riot ensued and many were killed. I was right in the middle of it and nearly died of a heart attack when a soldier, standing about ten feet away, pointed his automatic weapon directly at my head. But again, God was good. The soldier didn't fire and that indelible moment passed. One of the cameramen, however, got trampled, and all of us got banged up in the panic. Many, including me, were teargassed. After a couple of hours of this pandemonium, I managed to make it back to the Sheraton with the best news footage I have ever seen. This was major violence up close and personal, and it was an important international story. This time I knew I'd be leading Dan Rather's program.

Nope. In perhaps the most stunning thing that has ever happened to me, all the videotape was taken away from me and given to a big-name correspondent who was also slotted into *CBS Evening News* to report the lead story. That man never even left the hotel to *see* the story. Yet the CBS producers made him the star. In the parlance of network news, I had gotten "big-footed." To say I was angry is the understatement of the millennium.

I got the hell out of Argentina fast, landed in Miami, and raised a major ruckus at the CBS offices there. The bureau chief, my direct boss, told me to pipe down. I told him to, well, "rethink his tone." A few days later I was called back to New York for "consultations."

Fine. I returned to CBS headquarters on 57th Street, marched into Dan Rather's office, and let loose. "What the heck was this?" I asked. "What if a correspondent who wasn't even on the scene, *Dan*, stole your famous reporting during the Kennedy assassination? What would you have done? How can you abide stuff like this?"

Dan Rather was polite and I think I saw some sadness in his eyes. He said he'd look into it. I didn't believe him.

The next day I began investigating what happened to my missing report from El Salvador. I went down to the underground CBS archives and searched for hours. Finally, I spotted the label. I found the videotape! It was sitting there on a shelf gathering dust. I grabbed it and dropped it on the foreign editor's desk. Two weeks later my story ran on the weekend edition of CBS news. Nobody said a word about it except my father, who told me I was an idiot for even *going* to El Salvador.

After questioning the system in a very public and assertive way, I became a "dead man walking" at CBS News. Few people would even talk with me. Coincidentally, *TV Guide* was putting together a story on me and two other young reporters as "Future Superstars of Broadcast Journalism." The magazine had been impressed by the swiftness of my ascent from local news to the network level. CBS, of course, was less than thrilled with this development and downright anxious that I might tell all about the "big-footing" situation in Argentina. But I did not. For once in my life I kept my mouth shut and did not harpoon the company. I thought I was being sensible and I really hoped I was going to turn things around at CBS. To this day I don't know if I made the correct decision.

Before CBS and I parted company, I had one final inning with Dan Rather and his boys. For weeks I had basically sat in my New York office and done nothing, as no assignments came my way. But on a visit to Cape Cod, Massachusetts, I stumbled upon an amazing story. The tiny fishing village of Provincetown had become a gay mecca! Every Friday afternoon the ferry from Boston would dock, and hundreds of homosexual men, ready and willing to party, would disembark. The locals were stunned at first, then some of them got very angry. These were the disco days, and the weekend parties in the streets of Provincetown were intense and, to some observers, pretty shocking. The stage was set for a showdown.

To my surprise, CBS News okayed the story and off I went to Cape Cod accompanied by a photographer. On Friday night we used a hidden camera to shoot the wild activities. On Saturday we interviewed townspeople and some gays to get their perspectives.

In a nutshell the locals were very concerned that their kids were seeing stuff they should not be seeing, while the gays basically said, "Hey, look, we're entitled to vacation too. We can't help it if some people get crazy. The authorities should deal with them and leave the rest of us alone."

From my perspective, both sides had good points and were equally represented in my script. It was a terrific television story with fantastic video, and no other network had it. Once again I looked forward to being introduced by Dan Rather. Once again it didn't happen.

By this time I had had enough. I never got a straight answer as to why the story didn't run, but I knew the situation was hopeless. Years later a high-ranking CBS News guy told me the Provincetown report was simply too controversial and Dan, according to him, didn't want to take the kind of heat it would engender. What I didn't know at the time was that Rather was fighting his own fierce rearguard action against the remaining Cronkite faction inside CBS who despised him. So Dan didn't want to give the traditionalists any ammunition. Be that as it may, CBS killed a legitimate news story it never should have killed. What else is new?

A month later I left CBS to take an anchor/reporter job in Boston. Nineteen years after that, Dan Rather himself walked into the No Spin Zone.

That surprised me. Rather was on the broadcast circuit promoting a book, but a few weeks earlier I had conducted a fairly intense Zone interview with the chief of *60 Minutes*, Don Hewitt, who was also selling a book. During that conversation, I challenged Hewitt about the "soft" coverage I believe CBS had given Bill and Hillary Clinton. "Where was the investigative reporting?" I asked. Hewitt seemed to enjoy the joust, but there was no question that I felt CBS had gone into the tank with the Clintons.

So here comes Dan Rather into the Zone. I had seen him a few times over the years and we were always polite to each other. But I was still amazed that he, as the managing editor and the face of *CBS Evening News,* would *face* what he had to know was going to be some unfriendly fire. I didn't waste any time getting to the point.

O'REILLY: Why didn't you do any investigative reporting on campaign finance or Clinton's situations, the Chinese espionage, Janet Reno, Chuck LaBella, all of that?

RATHER: I think your definition of investigative reporting would pretty closely match mine—that is, not run-of-the-mill.

O'REILLY: Right, investigative reporting breaks news.

RATHER: I don't know whether we broke news or not. But it seems to me that on those things like campaign finance and Janet Reno we did as much or more than anybody else in the business.

O'REILLY: Can you give me one story you broke on campaign finance?

RATHER: I think I can. I think that when the—I'm drawing a blank on the man's name, the Hong Kong businessman—we were early in that story.

O'REILLY: That would be Riady, the Indonesian guy who was funneling money to the Democrats from the Chinese military.

RATHER: Yes. Jim Stewart broke several stories about the Riady case and we tried hard to interview him, recognizing that something didn't smell right about the story. Now, I won't say we nailed the story, we didn't. But we did do investigative reports on it, Bill.

O'REILLY: Okay, but when you interviewed Mr. Clinton himself in 1999—we have a transcript of the interview—you didn't ask him anything about the campaign finance stuff.

RATHER: Fair enough. Listen, if you consider that fair criticism, I have no argument with it. Look, I'm not a perfect interviewer.

O'REILLY: But it seems to me that with Mr. Clinton in that regard, CBS, NBC, ABC, and CNN were almost passive.

RATHER: I don't think that's right.

O'REILLY: Well, where did you guys break any stories? We were the ones who had Johnny Chung on first, Chuck LaBella [head campaign finance investigator for the Justice Department], and so on. Why are they coming on the *Factor* instead of the network news?

RATHER: Well, I don't know the answer to that question. I compliment you if you had them first. Tip of the Stetson to you. But this much I want clearly understood. We don't do it perfectly, we do it as well as we can do it. I accept your criticism. But what is not true is that there's an inner bias with us that goes easy on the Clintons and hard on somebody on the Republican side. The record does not show that. In my career I've tried to blow lights out on both sides of the street. Now, it's obviously your view that I don't blow the lights out as much on the Democratic side as the Republican side.

O'REILLY: I'm not saying that. What I am saying is that the networks and even the News Corporation [Fox]—they are the establishment now. Journalists are supposed to be outside the establishment, keeping an eye on it. My theory is, that is not happening, that there isn't serious investigative reporting going on at the network level, because the corporations have to do business with the powerful and they don't want to make enemies. We went through eight years of Mr. Clinton walking an ethical tightrope. We didn't see much from you guys.

RATHER: Well, there are two points here. I think the criticism that we weren't tough enough on Mr. Clinton is overstated, although I accept it. What I don't accept is that there's a left bias, a liberal bias.

O'REILLY: I believe there's an exclusionary bias rather than an ideological one.

RATHER: Well, I appreciate that. Now, the bigger point, which is as these companies get bigger that there's less investigative reporting. You're absolutely accurate about that, you're absolutely correct about that. It is by and large two things. One, money gets cut way back. I'm not the vice president in charge of excuses, but there are fewer resources today to do investigative reporting than there have ever been and—

O'REILLY: Let me stop you. I got nine people working for me. How many you got?

RATHER: Probably got ten.

O'REILLY: No, you've got a couple of hundred. We nailed Jesse Jackson to the wall because of his abuse of the nonprofit charity law. You guys and the other networks haven't touched it. Now the Chicago media is all over the story. Why wouldn't you pick up a story like that?

RATHER: If you're that far out front, what is there left for us to do? We don't do it perfectly, Bill. But we do a lot of investigative reporting. We have to make choices. Having said that, I will admit there is a kind of self-censorship that frequently goes on in big companies including News Corp. I do not exclude myself from that criticism.

O'REILLY: Do you really censor things, because I never do.

RATHER: I don't think that's true, Bill.

O'REILLY: If a story passes my desk and it's important to the American people, I do the story and I don't care who's involved.

RATHER: I don't believe that.

O'REILLY: Well, in the past five years I've taken on the biggest sacred cows in the country and I can prove it.

RATHER: I think that you do fresh reporting, aggressive reporting. Now, on Jesse Jackson, you don't think we did a very good job. You're entitled.

O'REILLY: You didn't do *anything*.

RATHER: I don't think we want to get bogged down in the small bramble bushes. The larger part of the forest is the self-censorship issue. It has to do with ratings. There are no excuses. What happens is, the pressure gets on to deliver an even bigger audience, and the belief begins to run strong that you can do it without the hard-nosed investigative stuff.

O'REILLY: Yes, but we have. We're killing the competition. My contention is this: that the powerful in this country protect each other. So let me ask you flat out: Do you think President Clinton is an honest man?

RATHER: Yes, I think he's an honest man.

O'REILLY: Even when he lied to the nation and to Jim Lehrer's face about the Lewinsky business?

RATHER: Who among us has not lied about something?

O'REILLY: Well, I haven't lied to anyone's face on national television. And I don't think you have either. Have you?

RATHER: I hope I never have.

O'REILLY: So how can you say Mr. Clinton is an honest man, then?

RATHER: Well, because I think he is. I think at core, he's an honest person. I know you have a different view. I know you think it rather astonishing anybody would say he's honest. But I think you can be an honest person and lie about any number of things.

O'REILLY: Really?

RATHER: I do.

O'REILLY: See, I want honest government across the board. When I see a president lying under oath, I see a guy undermining the justice system of this country.

RATHER: It's hard to be honest across the board.

O'REILLY: Let's take a look at some other stories. What about the Juanita Broaddrick thing?

RATHER: Juanita Broaddrick. To be perfectly honest, I don't remember all the details of that. But I will say that—and you can castigate me if you like—when the charge has something to do with somebody's private sex life, I would prefer to not run any of it. Now, I quite agree that critical mass was reached during the Clinton years, so it was unavoidable because it affected his performance in office. But I don't remember enough about Juanita Broaddrick.

O'REILLY: It was a rape charge.

RATHER: But basically her allegations.

O'REILLY: Well, Congressman Chris Shays [R-Connecticut] told us he interviewed Ms. Broaddrick's rape counselor and he believes her story. You respect Shays, right?

RATHER: Yes. But what you basically had was the Republicans trying to bring down Bill Clinton. That certainly was true just as the Democrats tried to bring down any number of Republicans. It's the way politics are played. So it was an organized campaign, and unfortunately for Bill Clinton and the country, some of it turned out to be true. But in that environment we are going to be very, very careful so as to not make any mistakes. We're not going to report the news the way a Republican pressure group wants us to report it, any more than we are going to report on unfounded allegations against George W. Bush. My attitude has always been, show me. You bring me documented evidence, you bring me some eyewitness testimony. And by the way I'll be sending my reporters out to find if it's a serious charge.

O'REILLY: What about when you're the subject of reporting? Do you think the press treated you fairly about the Democratic fundraiser you spoke at for your daughter?

RATHER: Yes, I was treated fairly. It was a dumb mistake, the worst kind of mistake. I am capable of being dumb as a sack full of hammers and this was one of those times.

O'REILLY: That really fed into the frenzy that Dan Rather is left-wing.

RATHER: Unfortunately, that's true.

Aside from an interview with Michael Kinsley, in which I told the *Slate* editor and liberal commentator to his face (and proved it) that he had attacked my honesty in a cowardly fashion, the Rather appearance sparked more news coverage and editorial comment than any other in the No Spin Zone. The whole country was talking about it.

The moment that really ignited interest was Rather's contention that an honest person will "lie about any number of things." Quite a few Americans didn't want to hear that kind of thinking from a journalist, especially in defense of the polarizing Bill Clinton. Wrote Tim Graham, *World* magazine's White House correspondent, "What was Rather thinking when he decided to go on Fox's *O'Reilly Factor*? Was he so desperate to sell a few more copies of his $25 idealistic book on *The American Dream* that he was willing to lower himself to suggesting that honesty is an ideal that doesn't really matter to him?"

Another scribe noted in the *National Review* that Rather's remarks proved that "you can be a network news grandee and bring out your moral relativism for all to see, unblushing and unashamed, when you have been cocooned among our agnostic elites for so long you think their attitudes are unremarkable."

The same writer likened the byplay between your humble correspondent and Dan Rather to the movie *The Cincinnati Kid*. I guess I was playing the Steve McQueen part and Dan was the elder statesman played by Edward G. Robinson. At least I *hope* that's what the writer had in mind.

Anyway, when my assistant buzzed me the day after the Rather interview and announced that Dan Rather was on the line, I was prepared for the worst. But Rather was complimentary and told me I did my job. The same job I tried to do for him all those years ago.

Life is like that: You never know what will come around. I have never disliked Dan Rather and have followed his career closely. That interview with him is one of my all-time favorites and I respect him for engaging the Zone. What we talked about really matters. The conversation vividly demonstrates the difference between us. I am a journalist who insists on honest government; I'm an absolutist (some say fanatic) in that way. Lie, cheat, steal in the public arena—I'm gonna let you have it and I don't care who you are.

Dan Rather is more of a pragmatist. He indeed has seen it all and is willing to tolerate far more shenanigans than I am. He understands that a certain amount of corruption is built into the system and is willing to play by those rules. I am not. There is no room for *any* public dishonesty in the No Spin Zone and we will expose it with vigor. I'll leave it to you to decide which journalistic entity is more relevant in the first part of this new century. The Zone is there and *CBS Evening News* is there. America is all about having choices. And one of the choices each of us has to make is whether or not to put our beliefs on the line and defend them in the toughest circumstance.

Do you hear that, Hillary Clinton?

CHAPTER FOURTEEN

It Would Take a Village to Drag

Hillary into the No Spin Zone

ISSUE 14: Dodging the tough interviews

THE OPPONENT: Hillary Clinton, senator from New York

Who's afraid of the No Spin Zone? It's a question people always ask. I've already mentioned a couple of persistent no-shows. Jesse Jackson, of course. From stage left, Al Gore would not venture in, and from stage right, Republican Congressman Tom DeLay said no to the Zone after we criticized his fund-raising techniques. Attorneys General Reno and Ashcroft have both demurred. And Hillary and Bill Clinton loathe the Zone with all their being since, to quote *TV Guide* about me, I'm "championing the regular guy against entrenched power and lying sacks of spin."

And I firmly believe the cowards are the long-term losers. Call me a conceited dreamer, but I believe Al Gore would have won the election had he faced me on television and acquitted himself well. If the former vice president had parried my questions with intelligent and straightforward answers, thousands of undecided Floridians would have either seen the interview or heard about it from friends. That would have translated into some votes. You see, most viewers respect people who entertain hard questions even if they don't like their answers. After Al Sharpton appeared in the Zone, I received scores of letters praising his courage. And many of them came from viewers who had never before found anything praise-worthy about Reverend Sharpton.

But Al Gore wouldn't risk a no spin interview in which he might have to explain things like why he was so opposed to public school vouchers—which would give poor families a chance to move their kids out of poorly performing public schools—while sending his own children to private schools. I'm certain ol' Al didn't want to try to tell me why he changed his long-standing po-sitions on abortion, gun control, and tobacco. Al Gore knew that his rehearsed stock answers, the kind he used on the elite media, would not have been kindly received in the Zone.

Hillary Clinton has also avoided me, but her campaign was successful. I have to admit that astounded me. During her run for the Senate, Hillary shot down all one-on-one interviews with jour-nalists she could not control. Even the legendary WNBC-TV po-litical reporter Gabe Pressman, who has interviewed *everybody*, got the big raspberry from Hillary until safely after her election.

NBC newsman Tim Russert did get a few haymakers in dur-ing one of the televised debates with her opponent, Congressman Rick Lazio, but other than that, Hillary wasn't verbally challenged during her campaign for the Senate.

Not that I didn't try. My staff called her office nearly every day, and hysterical laughter could often be heard through the phone. Hillary enter O'Reilly's No Spin Zone? Yeah, and in the next seg-ment Yasir Arafat will be bar mitzvahed.

Meanwhile, Mrs. Clinton worked very hard. I give her that.

She appeared in all counties of the state and met with every special interest group she could find.

Sometimes she worked *too* hard. Speaking to a "gay pride" event, she suggested, according to *The New Republic*, that participants should show up as their "favorite issue." I quote: "Now, for some people, that may be prescription drugs. You know, for others it can be sensible gun safety measures, or choice, or the environment. I wouldn't mind seeing a number of trees going to the polls on November 7!"

What?

Many Americans know that I have badgered Hillary to enter the Zone. Sometimes badgering works, but not with her. So I had no choice but to call her out. Shortly before the historical November 2000 election, I wrote a public "memo" to Hillary Clinton in my syndicated column.

"Well, just four more weeks until voting day, Hillary, and you've cracked the 50 percent voter approval rating. You lead Rick Lazio by about ten points in the polls and things are lookin' very well indeed. Your strategy of running around the state of New York talking in generalities seems to be working. And the fact that the notoriously vicious New York press has given you a giant air kiss is simply incredible.

"Especially since you have given the media your middle finger for the past sixteen months. Your press conferences are tightly controlled, and face-to-face interviews with you are almost impossible. Your Praetorian Guard of Secret Service agents makes it impossible for the media to get near you, and your highly paid advisers reject almost every print and television request for a sit-down.

"In the past this would have gotten a big Bronx cheer from New York voters, but now the Bronx is firmly in your corner.

That's because many of the poor who inhabit the outer boroughs of New York City feel the government owes them plenty. And you promise to *deliver plenty*. Also, there are hundreds of thousands of new naturalized citizens in New York and many of them love you. They could not care less about your opponent.

"As we all know, Americans do either love you or hate you, and right now you are getting sugar from the majority of New Yorkers. Again, that's a bit strange because you haven't really done anything in the public arena and New Yorkers demand performance on the field and success in the clutch. Your two major issues are education and health care. They are nice issues, Hil, but they are a bear to deal with, as you know. You oversaw the educational programs in Arkansas for eight years while Bill was governor. In all that time Arkansas went from 49th to 49th in the national educational rankings. Thank God for Mississippi.

"And then there was the health care ordeal. Bill put you in charge of his health revolution and, please forgive me for saying this, Hillary, you turned it into a catastrophe. I know, I know, you learned a lot in the process. But people in Romania were mocking us. People who still believe that putting leeches on your body is a great prescription were saying, 'You know, I think I'll stay with the leeches. They're a lot simpler to figure out than Hillary's plan.'

"But as Bill Murray once said in the great movie *Meatballs*, 'It just doesn't matter.' Your run for the Senate is not based on achievement or vision or anything but naked power and fame. And you're winning! Isn't New York a great place?

"In the debate with Rick Lazio you sounded a bit tentative. You also looked a little tight. But then Mr. Lazio did you an enormous favor—he invaded your personal space with his soft-money challenge. Thousands of women who resent men throwing their weight around did not like that one bit. And your poll numbers went up. Who could have predicted that? Not me.

"Hollywood is thrilled that you may be the next senator from New York and this is great. The stars provide money, moral support, and the glamour that the New York press and many voters can't get enough of. I mean Rosie O'Donnell is in heaven! I hope we'll be seeing you and your mom back on *Rosie* again soon. I'm sure we won't be seeing Rick Lazio and his mom—even though he grew up not too far away from Rosie on Long Island.

"Dave Letterman's guys wrote you some pretty snappy material the last time you visited his program and that was nifty. You came across charming and witty. Maybe you really *are* like that, but how would anyone know? You never speak spontaneously and you never answer direct questions on the campaign trail. You have your comments memorized and the less said about anything else the better.

"So I'm liking your chances, Hil. If New Yorkers are for you at this point after watching you for the past sixteen months, then, hey, you've got it. Very cleverly you campaigned on the taxpayer's dime, used the White House for quid pro quo campaign contributions, and somehow convinced the media to give you a free ride. Brilliantly done, Mrs. Clinton!

"The Senate will be just great. You'll vote straight Democratic on every issue, serve on a few committees, and maybe sponsor some expensive legislation. And the big prize might be only four years away. It's a great life, Hillary, and you're just getting going. Please say hello from me to Bill if you ever see him, and if you ever need a house sitter in Chappaqua, you know I am available.

"Your pal, Bill O'Reilly"

Sadly, I never received a reply from Hillary Clinton. It's been a long time now and nary a word. Why, if she would talk with me, I'd even give her a copy of this book!

Rejected, I have to take my consolation in fantasies. Each night while lying in bed I visualize the interview. At last we are together in the Zone. Her pantsuit is peach, her hair perfect, and she's backed by five Secret Service guys with weapons at the ready. I smile. I speak softly. I ask the following questions:

O'REILLY: Madam Senator, while your husband was governor of Arkansas, you made big money in the commodities market, turning a $1,000 investment into something close to $100,000. According to the *Journal of Economics and Statistics*, the odds of that happening are 250 million to 1! So, uh, how did it happen? [I feign some nervousness here.]

HILLARY:

O'REILLY: In the Whitewater fiasco your billing records disappeared from the computer system of your employer the Rose law firm. Then two years later they mysteriously turned up inside the White House living quarters with your fingerprints on them. How did *that* happen?

HILLARY:

O'REILLY: Would you like a glass of water, Mrs. Clinton? . . . No? . . . Fine. Let's continue. How do you justify sending Chelsea to private school while opposing vouchers for poor parents who may want to send their kids to private school?

HILLARY:

O'REILLY: A Mars bar, Mrs. Clinton? Snickers? . . . Okay, just asking. What about this: Forty-five minutes after the suicide of your friend White House counsel Vince Foster, you called your assistant Maggie Williams and sent her to Foster's office. Why?

HILLARY:

O'REILLY: Another White House counsel, Bernie Nussbaum, removed files from Foster's office and refused to hand them over to investigators, citing attorney-client privilege. Did you ever talk with Nussbaum about those files?

HILLARY:

O'REILLY: To continue, it is estimated that you used millions of taxpayer dollars to campaign in New York State. You often flew to campaign stops aboard air force jets and logged the trips under your duties as First Lady. Was this fair?

HILLARY: *(standing up quickly and snapping)* You can shoot him now, boys . . .

The pistols are aimed, and I then wake up in a cold sweat.

I have this dream over and over again. But the worst part is, I have at least ten more questions ready when the firing begins.

Of all the people in the United States, Hillary Clinton would be the last one to consent to an appearance in the No Spin Zone. Someday, somehow, I believe I may get a shot at her husband, Al Gore, and Jesse Jackson. But it would take a village of marauding Goliaths to drag Hil into the Zone. As George Bush the elder might say, "She's not gonna do it."

I wish she would. We could put it on pay-per-view. Don King would do anything to promote this. The Vegas guys would go wild. Please, Mrs. Clinton, take your seat in the No Spin Zone. Do it for the children and for immature adults like me.

CHAPTER FIFTEEN

No Spin Viewers

ISSUE 15: Not liking O'Reilly

THE OPPONENTS: Regular folks

ABDI: O'Reilly, I don't like the way you disrupt your guests. Please get some help from Larry King. He might teach you how to interview.

O'REILLY: I doubt it, Abdi. But then again, you never know. By the way, do you think Hillary and Al Gore are afraid to go on Larry's broadcast?

MICHELE: O'Reilly, I quit watching the *Factor* because I find you so egotistical. So now my mother calls me every evening to tell me what I missed. I don't know which is worse.

O'REILLY: Michele, Michele, Michele . . . listen to your mom. She obviously knows what's best.

Some weeks, more than 25,000 letters arrive in the Zone. They come from people all over the world sounding off about everything you can think of. And one of the most popular topics is . . . me.

How could such a shy guy generate so much, uh, feeling? I can't figure it out.

The feeling comes in all shades. We get plenty of good, complimentary mail, and I try to answer as much of it as I can. The negative stuff is separated into a special pile. Because of time constraints, I selectively respond to both friendly and unfriendly fire on my television program. But in this chapter I want to deal directly with some of the unfavorable letters. Here's why: Many of the pans are full of no spin. The Zone likes that.

The negative mail divides neatly into two camps. Those who don't approve of my positions on issues, and those who simply don't approve of me in my entirety. Let's begin with a correspondent from Vermont named Don: "Mr. O'Reilly, every time I stumble across your program, I am amazed how rude and obnoxious you are. And no there is no context in which it is appropriate. A typical rude American attitude. Yes, I am American."

Don joins legions of people all over the world who see me as "rude." But I can explain. The No Spin Zone shuts down people who don't directly answer the questions or purposely distort the facts. In order to impose the Zone rules, I have to interrupt when a guest begins to meander or, well, lie.

There are three reasons for this. First, I don't want to waste your time. Far too many TV interviewers allow their guests to blather on about nothing. Second, facts are facts—I have them in hand, and if the guest denies those facts, verbal confrontation immediately ensues. Finally, television is now run by computers. I have only so much time for each interview before the commercial break automatically appears on your screen. The machines have taken over. I *have* to interrupt to stay on time. It breaks my heart.

I'm spinning. It doesn't break my heart. I want people to GET TO THE POINT. I want them to be pithy. I want them to tell you the truth or what they think is the truth. I don't want bloviating, equivocating, or weaseling of any kind. Chatus interruptus is sometimes desperately needed on television.

So, Don is right. Sometimes I am rude, but I don't mean it to be offensive. It's just the rules of the game. The Zone rules.

James from Ohio is next up. "Sir, to be fair to you I watched three weeks' worth of the *Factor* to get a full flavor of your content and style. In all honesty I must admit that your program is a disgrace to 'real' journalism. Your bullying style is neither effective nor admirable. Did you ever see Walter Cronkite point his finger in someone's face? Shame on you."

The clue in this letter is the mention of Cronkite. Chances are the writer is a senior citizen who enjoyed ol' Walter's calm demeanor as he read the day's headlines each night on *CBS Evening News*. In England such activity is honestly called what it is: news reading. Walter Cronkite did not express his opinions. He wanted to appear objective and credible and fair.

What I do is completely different. I *analyze* the news. I am the op-ed page of television.

Many viewers don't understand this concept because it is brand-new in prime time. The *Factor* is not a hard news broadcast. It is opinion and analysis. But when I give an opinion, the word "commentary" usually appears on your TV screen. We try to guide our viewers through the No Spin Zone because we realize that we are different. Some people can handle it, some people cannot.

And some people like Celia from California are in the middle.

"O'Reilly, it seems pretty clear to me that you are quite proud of your bombastic, interruptive manner. I agree with several of your positions, but our country already suffers from so much incivility in the media. Must you add to it in the name of no spin?"

Celia is correct. I *am* proud of the Zone, and I don't believe we are disrespectful to anyone. We are *direct*. I fully realize that some nonconfrontational viewers (PBS watchers?) find this offensive. But most of our guests and viewers return. Only a very few interview subjects, like Clinton adviser Rahm Emmanuel and Mary Frances Berry of the NAACP, have stalked off in a huff. The Zone is a serious place. Every day we deal with important issues and we follow the credo of the legendary band the Talking Heads: "This ain't no party, this ain't no disco, this ain't no foolin' around."

Journalism is supposed to be tough. The truth is not easily exposed when propagandists are paid huge sums of money to spin lies and deceit. Celia is watching this all unfold and some of it is unsettling to her. That's okay—unsettling can be good.

And then there's Norman, also from California. "Mr. O'Reilly, I watch you on TV and have read your book [*The O'Reilly Factor: The Good, the Bad, and the Completely Ridiculous in American Life*]. I expect that soon you will come out with music. A song something like 'I'm marvelous, I'm wonderful to see.' Why are you so conceited?"

This is another very common theme in the negative mailbox. And I have to admit that I am not a humble guy. But that's not my fault, as all of my ancestors were conceited louts. I need your sympathy, Norman, not your scorn. I need a government program to save me.

But here's some no-spin on Norman's observation. Anyone—and I mean *anyone*—who delivers a strong opinion in America is going to be labeled an egomaniac. That's just how it is. In many parts of this country it is considered extremely ill-mannered to voice a dissenting opinion. You'll ruin Thanksgiving dinner. You'll start a fight in the bar. You'll *offend* somebody. Dating Rosie O'Donnell or falling into a pit of vipers is not the number one fear among Americans, public speaking is. The country founded on freedom of speech is populated by human beings who are often deathly afraid of speaking up in front of a crowd.

Your mother probably told you—mine told me—that you should never talk about religion or politics. And what am I doing every night? Making a career out of talking about religion and politics and everything else on the planet. For that, I take a massive amount of heat from people like Norm. Fair enough. But like Harry Truman, I can stick it out in the kitchen.

Behind the refrigerator in that kitchen is often somebody like Barbara from Phoenix, who finds me personally offensive. "Mr. O'Reilly, you are rude, crude and unattractive. Nothing personal, just the facts as I see them."

Nooooo. Nothing *personal*, Barb. And if you think I'm unattractive on the tube, you should see me without makeup. Dogs howl. Bats fly in the daylight. Blowfish giggle.

Abdi, who lives in Houston, agrees with Barbara but goes further, offering me some professional advice. "O'Reilly, I don't like the way you disrupt your guests. Please get some help from Larry King. He might teach you how to interview."

I doubt it, Abdi. But then again, you never know. However, I'm not sure my ego could take instruction from Larry. And Michele from Michigan would second that. "O'Reilly, I quit watching the *Factor* because I find you so egotistical. So now my mother calls me every evening to tell me what I missed. I don't know which is worse."

Michele, Michele, Michele. Listen to your mom. She knows

what's best for you even if you don't. And I am saying that in all humility.

Gina lives in Ohio, but I suspect she and Michele hang out. "O'Reilly, let me see if I have this right—if you make enough money you can be arrogant and scream at the people on your program. Why do you make a fool out of yourself?"

I don't know, Gina, I just don't know. As for the "screaming," it is called "passionate discussion." Just because a voice is raised doesn't mean there's "screaming." I like to see emotion in a person. I am tired of zombies doing the news. ARE YOU HEARING ME, GINA? Whoops. Sorry, Gina. I bet you never thought a book would yell at you.

And then there are the ideologues, the viewers on both the left and the right who absolutely go nuts when you criticize their "guys." Thousands of letters poured into the Zone after we exposed Jesse Jackson's nonprofit tax returns. The documents showed that very little donated money was going for charitable work.

That teed Curtis from Los Angeles off big-time. "I can't believe a television network would put someone like you, O'Reilly, on the air. You are a racist and you can't furnish evidence to dispute this fact."

Ah, the old race card. It is alive and well in America. You can thank folks like Jesse Jackson and David Duke for that. Forget the merits of our investigation, I am a racist for even bringing up the subject. Well, Curtis, all I can say is that you are wrong and your criticism is cheap. Drop that line of nonsense and debate the facts. You'll be a better man for it.

And how about the Clintonistas? Wooo. They don't like your humble correspondent. I designated Brian in Colorado to speak for them. "Mr. O'Reilly, the pit-bull-like ferocity with which you attack the Clintons has strayed into the area of irrationality. There comes a time when investigative reporting becomes a witch-hunt. Be a journalist, not a lynch mob organizer."

What can I say, Brian? Bill Clinton will go down in history as one of the most corrupt presidents of all time. I reported that. And there's still much more to come. Keep watching.

And of course there is thunder from the right. Tammy from Tennessee is fired up because I believe homosexuals should have equal protection under the law. "O'Reilly, why do you hate Christians? I believe the Bible is the word of God, and I take it literally. Homosexuality is an abomination to the Lord. Why are you so intolerant?"

Tammy, it is your right to believe in the Bible and live according to it. It is not your right to *impose* that belief on anyone else. I happen to believe that all Americans have a right to make a living and have a lifestyle free from religious judgment. As long as gays or any other group do not intrude on you, they should be left alone. Let God sort the private stuff out. He is smart enough to do it right.

There's something very peculiar about the negative letters, by the way. As you can see from the above sampling, I get it from both sides—and each side is firmly convinced that I'm the enemy. How does that happen?

Richard from Oklahoma puts me somewhere to the left of the ACLU: "O'Reilly, you sneer at those who do not share your liberal views. You would make a good member of the super-liberal gang headed by Al Hunt and Margaret Carlson."

Not so fast, Richard. Alan in Connecticut takes issue with your missive. "Mr. O'Reilly, how dare you consider yourself a journalist? Your smug attitude and unconditional love for the Republican Party is obvious."

Is it really, Alan? Here's the no spin truth: I am an independent. I vote for the most honest and most effective problem-solver in the running. The politician I've most admired in my lifetime is Bobby Kennedy, a Democrat. The politician I least respect is Bill Clinton, a Democrat.

Okay, test me . . . go through my beliefs and come up with the appropriate ism.

- I believe that the federal government wastes a huge amount of the people's money and that most politicians buy votes with entitlement promises.

- I believe that global warming is real.

- I believe that the green movement has hurt America because it has shut down responsible energy exploration.

- I don't believe in the death penalty.

- I would not outlaw abortion, but I would restrict it and encourage Americans to see this ghastly procedure as a human rights issue.

- I believe in stringent control of hard drugs, but I would decriminalize marijuana use.

- I would "suggest" that the automakers develop cars and trucks that would be far more fuel-efficient than they are today. (If they don't, the government ought to slap a huge tax on them.)

- I would order the Department of Energy to strictly monitor any kind of energy price collusion or gouging—and impose massive fines on any company found guilty of these crimes.

- I would have the federal government negotiate discounted drug prices with pharmaceutical companies so that there could be an affordable Medicare drug benefit. These manufacturers should be pressured to be "generous" in their pricing and rewarded with tax incentives for complying.

- I believe America should maintain the most powerful armed forces in the world and develop a missile shield if the technology is feasible.

- I would eliminate the payroll tax and institute a national sales tax to cover Social Security and Medicare. The sales tax would slide depending on need. Those Americans who saved would be rewarded. The poorest would have more cash in their pockets.

- I support setting up federal prison work camps on federal land in Alaska for violent offenders. Murder, rape, hard-drug dealing, and gun crimes would be punished at the federal level—taking the massive expense and chaos away from the states. These federal prisons would be run military style, and the violent convicts would in effect be banished from society.

- I believe our government should place the U.S. military on the border with Mexico to stabilize the illegal immigrant and drug smuggling problems. The military would back up the Border Patrol but would have arrest powers, requiring that the posse comitatus law be changed.

- In conjunction with strict border enforcement, the USA should set up a "guest worker" program if the Mexican government would cooperate. U.S. companies and individuals that need labor would be able to participate in the program. But it would be administered in an orderly manner and taxes would be paid.

Okay, so what do these beliefs make me? To what party or ideology do I belong? Tell me—I'd like to know.

Maybe Tony who lives in Texas has the right take on it. "Mr. O'Reilly, how dare you report the news from both sides. Who do you think you are asking Jesse Jackson and others to answer for their actions? Keep up the good work."

Millions of Americans like Tony get it. They know exactly what's going on in the No Spin Zone. They see that we provide solutions to problems, not just vacant looks and general criticisms. They know that rank partisanship and irresponsible governance appall us. That's why the Zone has become a power in America.

The intelligentsia *hates* that. They loathe the fact that the No Spin Zone has taken root. Magazines like *New York* and *The New Republic* spend an inordinate amount of time trying to convince their readers that your humble correspondent is, in varying degrees, a nitwit, poseur, or worse. *The New Republic* even tried to portray me as one of *them*. Yikes! "O'Reilly's insistence that he's an outsider isn't an affectation; it's delusional. Although his biography offers obvious proof to the contrary . . . he sees himself as separate from an alien, hostile elite."

My biography offers obvious proof to the contrary? Talk about delusional. The writer has no idea what the social or economic climate was in Levittown, New York, in the 1960s—nor does he care. The only thing he and others like him care about is trying to slap a hypocrisy tag on anyone who successfully challenges the media elite.

But the popular media are starting to come around. It took a while and we weathered some withering criticism, but in June 2001 I appeared on the cover of *TV Guide*, causing weeping and the gnashing of teeth in many quarters. The headline of the article read, "Bill O'Reilly isn't afraid of anybody. From the most prominent politicians to the most respected journalists . . . O'Reilly holds everybody accountable. For soft reporting, for abuses of power, even for social snobbery. The man who was once an outsider in television now has everyone's ear and he won't be ignored."

Not quite. The truth is, I'm still an outsider in television and in the corridors of power no matter what anyone says. I am not and never will be a member of "the club." It is the regular folks who have made the No Spin Zone and me successful. Folks like Randy from Washington State, who wrote, "Mr. O'Reilly, you have single-handedly revived my interest in the news. I admire anyone who has the guts to appear in the No Spin Zone. Thanks for exposing corruption and hypocrisy."

You're welcome, Randy. Thanks for appreciating the Zone.

CHAPTER SIXTEEN

Caution: You Are About to

Enter a No Spin Zone

This final chapter is between you and me. Man to woman. Man to man. Man to kid. The question in play is a most important one: Should you establish your own personal No Spin Zone?

And don't react too quickly . . . The answer is not as obvious as you might think.

It's a question that only you can answer. To do so, let's imitate Benjamin Franklin's approach to making a decision: We'll make a list of pros and cons and then try to balance them out.

Pro: A personal No Spin Zone will save you time, money, and frustration. It will allow you to make value judgments based upon hard facts and evidence. And—provided that you keep an open mind and examine all available credible data—you'll be comfortable with your conclusions on most matters.

Here's the key that unlocks the Zone: the ability to be rigorous with yourself in always challenging your initial thoughts and conclusions. The Zone is no place for zealots, lemmings, or weak-minded followers. It is a state of mind that demands the discipline of clear thinking and the flexibility to change that thinking should the evidence dictate. Summing up, the No Spin Zone is *not* an easy place to be.

Why? Because it's far easier to let others form your opinions. You then don't have to exercise your brain cells and the crowd will readily accept you. Politicians, commentators, and others vying to fill your head space are eager to supply you with particular points of view. And increasingly, many Americans are buying into viewpoints that crush independent thinking. Why think when media talking heads and newspaper columnists will do that for you? After all, aren't these people "experts"?

Well, no, they are not. At least most of them aren't. There are no experts when it comes to making personal decisions. That's your own private domain. Sure, nobody is right all the time and you won't be either. We are all occasionally defeated on the field of logic. But take your shot at forming your own personal philosophy. It's actually fun and satisfying to develop a code of behavior and a clear thinking pattern. Don't let pinheads, even smart pinheads, do your thinking for you. Ben Franklin would be appalled if you did that.

Con: The biggest negative about establishing a personal No Spin Zone is that it will alienate some people you may not want to alienate. Here's the best warning I can give you: Don't be like me! You don't have to confront the spinners head-on, as I do. It's my job to be a pain in the butt or a loudmouth boor (I put that in for the readers in Berkeley, California, and Cambridge, Massachusetts). But you can use diplomacy in your personal Zone; you can conduct yourself with measured authority. Also, I have only an hour each day to get my point across—you have a lifetime. You can use finesse in the Zone and you can outsmart the spinners of this world.

But why bother? I'm talking about a lot of concentrated, continuing work. And even with that you are going to butt heads with people, no matter how diplomatic you are. It's sad but true: Many Americans resent any kind of intellectual challenge. Question some dopey statement they've made, and their response will likely be a personal attack on you.

But here's some no spin magic potion. *Avoid those people*. That's part of setting up a personal No Spin Zone: avoiding cretins whom you cannot possibly win over. Very few people have actual power over you; you can safely ignore those who don't. Smile at them and wave as you walk away. There are more than 6 billion persons on the planet. You can afford to lose the hopeless and the misguided.

So how about it? Pro or con? Of course I am the gatekeeper of the No Spin Zone and its biggest fan. There are huge upsides in setting up your own personal Zone. You will become more aware, exercising your God-given talents of perception and reasoning. You will begin to pay closer attention to the world around you. That leads to an improved ability to seize opportunities and avoid costly mistakes. You are far more likely to reject foolish, dangerous people who can betray your trust and dampen your spirit. You will take no individuals or issues for granted because you will be constantly making decisions based upon facts and life experience. In sum you will be more alive, and this will add tremendous power to your life.

Most of my acquaintances tell consistent tales of woe. They are always being taken advantage of or bamboozled. They feel victimized all the time. I'm sure you know people like this. But after you set up a personal No Spin Zone, you will learn not to tolerate victimizers or charlatans or liars or manipulators. First off, you can just refuse to associate with them. And if that doesn't work and they are still having an impact on your life, call them out verbally. Do this only when it is absolutely necessary, but you have a perfect right to be fool free.

If solicitors call my home, for example, I tell them within ten seconds that I do not do business on the phone—they can send me something if they like. Then I hang up. Rude? No. The *call* is intrusive and rude.

Another example is that I have instituted the two-call rule in my personal Zone. If I call a person twice and don't receive a call back, that relationship is over. I leave a short message saying that I will not be calling again. If it's a business matter, I turn the thing over to my attorney (an old friend I trust). If I absolutely have to reach someone for business, I call his or her secretary and set up a phone appointment. I ask for an exact time when I can talk to the person. If the secretary is unwilling to do that, I know that the business arrangement, whatever it is, will not work.

Other Zone commandments: If I've made a restaurant reservation, I expect it to be honored within fifteen minutes. Same with a doctor's appointment. The physician's time is valuable but so is mine and so is yours. Being on time and honoring your word are signs of respect. I want to deal only with people who are respectful of others, even in a casual setting such as a restaurant. Be aware of how others are treating you and question that treatment if you feel it isn't square. That's all part of a no spin life.

Now, you don't have to be as rigid as I am in my Zone, and you can come up with your own set of rules. But believe me, nobody wastes my time. And no one cons me. I have a good broker, lawyer, taxman, and great friends, many of whom I have known for most of my life. I brook no lies, no deceit, no insincerity. I am almost the same off the air as I am on the air. Is that frightening or what?

But the Zone has worked for me. I have a good life. I am not a victim or a victimizer. I have never owed anybody any money and I fulfill my obligations. I have two basic reasons for trying to lead a no spin life: My time and my honor are valuable to me. Very valuable.

Hey, I probably don't have to convince you—I already know you're a Zone-friendly person. How do I know that? Because you've stuck with me and my ideas to the end of this book. I hope you have enjoyed the journey through these pages, and I am honored that you have taken the time to consider what I have to say.

I can guarantee you that life in the No Spin Zone is never boring, usually fun, and always challenging. While millions of others are indeed spinning their wheels, those in the Zone are forging ahead, making progress in their lives without getting dizzy and disoriented.

That's because we're on solid ground. That's the true beauty of the No Spin Zone: It most often leaves you feeling clear and content at the end of the day. You have time for the important things like family and friends. The Zone is a code, a lifestyle, a complete no-frills thought process.

Believe me when I tell you I believe what I'm saying, and am in the Zone for the long run. In fact, even longer . . . because I've set aside these words to be engraved on my tombstone:

"HE'LL NEVER SPIN IN HIS GRAVE."

Here's how I discovered Bill O'Reilly. It's a Tale of Two Bills.

It was winter '98. I was home in Kansas City writing a book—and largely ignoring the media. A sense of Bill Clinton as predatory, mendacious, and ultimately self-destructive simmered on my back-burner brain. The Clinton-Lewinsky scandal broke. I devoted TV time to the event and watched the mainstream media spin. The circus atmosphere and exploitative coverage did not divert or alter my feeling that Bill Clinton was culpable and had to pay.

I was outraged by Clinton's actions and enraged by his henchmen's lies and rationalizations. The TV coverage was long on detail and two-party rancor and dissembling. I wanted to find a media guide who would decelerate the spin and address the details and personalities in more depth—from a standpoint of committed rectitude. I flipped channels until I found Bill O'Reilly.

I knew bupkes about O'Reilly. I was news-channel challenged and Internet-ignorant and media demagnetized. O'Reilly was a giddy non sequitur. Kansas winters are cooooold. I went into hibernation with my book and nightly viewings of *The O'Reilly Factor.*

O'Reilly french-fried and fricasseed Bill Clinton. O'Reilly turned Clinton apologists apoplectic. He mauled Mike McCurry and lashed Lanny Davis. He julienned the juvenile antics of Bad Bill Clinton and critiqued the cost of his priapic presidency. He operated on optimum outrage and sustained his rage through to impeachment. He nailed the missteps and excesses of Clinton's opponents and speared *their* spin machines. He soldiered for Truth. He waxed pissed, brash, irate, rude, and wrathful. He fought the public apathy that kept Clinton in office. He inoculated himself with an antidote for Clinton Fatigue Syndrome and tracked the residual scandals when the mainstream media moved on. He fought knowledgeably and hard. He pounded on partisan bias and lobbed Left-Right logic into the lurch.

I stayed with *The Factor* post-Clinton. I developed a thesis about O'Reilly. I made him as the A-prototype fifty-year-old American male at century's end. He's running on equal parts patriotism and skepticism. He's got Faith and Reason tenuously reconciled. He grew up at great cost and thus deplores bad behavior. He lives in a lunatic TV world that forces him to gorge on every last crumb of the current and always fluctuating American cultural scene *and* turn it into high-rated narrative—a burden of transient minutiae that no sane person should bear. He's a truth guy spinning his wheels then—culling, sifting, analyzing, *reacting*. It's the pure definition of TV insanity—but he's spun himself out of the crowd.

O'Reilly confronted this lunacy. He wrote a mega-best-selling memoir/rant called *The O'Reilly Factor* and followed it up with the book you've just read. It's better than the *Factor* book. It's the TV show synthesized and refined.

It's got the O'Reilly bombast, wit, and persuasive argument

sans commercial interruptions, O'Reilly's interruptions, and the dud guests who occasionally limp or charge into the No Spin Zone and stink the place up with specious rhetoric. It's free of timed segment strictures and the need to stay hotly topical to goose the Nielsen stats. It's got O'Reilly well matched across the issue spectrum, good *Factor* exchanges recounted verbatim, and O'Reilly with the first and last words—expanding and encapsulating the dialogue unrestricted by TV demands. The book displays the range of his moral concerns and commitment to Reason. The book displays his grandstanding egomania—which will sell *beaucoup* copies to folks who watch *The Factor* to boo him. The book pinpoints the fatuous nature of liberal-conservative discourse—as O'Reilly jumps around the ideological map, rags the Right and lops the Left. The book shows us how much our society is ruled by blindly followed and reflexive political classification, and holds up the tyrannical and crooked to scrutiny and scorn.

You get the guy on TV on the page. It's not quite O'Reilly Unchained—he still says "bull" instead of the more persuasive and declarative "bullshit"—but it's O'Reilly more fully dimensionalized. *And* it's a primer on why you tune in to watch him.

He wants the best for you—but he doesn't need to know you or need you to love him. His middle-brow cultural tastes play well in Des Moines. He thinks he's the greatest thing on God's green earth—but the women in his life and half his viewers half-smile and half-wince at the notion. He believes in human dignity and the sanctity of life. He likes women—beyond the standard sexual equation. He reins in the untoward aspects of his personality—because he knows that the social contract demands it. He whines about his taxes at great length and would be well served to shut up and howl at the jumbo coin he's making. He's the Irish blowhard at the Blarney Stone bar on Forty-eighth and Eighth. He's got opinions on every topic—but he's never drunk, he's omnivorously well briefed, and he's right 80 percent of the time. He won't talk about his wife and kid on the air. He doesn't yuk on command when celebrities drop one-liners. His personal monologues run lengthy. He listens well one-on-one. He needs to tamp down his stress level sixteen notches. He knows we're all here on the Good Lord's dime. He's the most articulate rebuke to moral relativism on the field today.

Here's more on the Two Bills. Post-Clinton America is a spin zone spinning in the winds of Bad Bill's reign of corruption. A big theme of the No Spin Zone is the heavily accruing cost of Clinton's legacy of personal default and the way this ethical relinquishment pervades our society. O'Reilly mercilessly attacks the culture of excuse-making and individual and group capitulation. He sees rationalized grievance-mongering and the disappearance of personal honor and responsibility zooming to epidemic proportions. He deftly tracks a strain of the virus to the Clinton Spin. O'Reilly makes doctrinaire liberals, dubious humanists, and proponents and exploiters of racial conflict—black and white—squirm. He exposes the bonehead Left-Right political line that defines man-in-the-street politics and media discourse. He's equally at home bashing heedless supporters of Jesse Jackson and right-wing religious nuts.

I told some folks at a Manhattan party that I dug O'Reilly. The dinner table froze. Jaws gaped. A fork dropped. I got the split-second reassessment of reflex orthodoxy. Who's this guy? Is he a gun freak? What's his stand on the biting issues of the day that *we* stand united on? *Bill O'Reilly?!?* He shouts, he cuts people off, he wanted to pull that dung-flecked painting of the Virgin Mary from the Brooklyn Museum, which is sooooooooo uncool. Bill O'Reilly . . . he's not one of *us*.

No, he's not. Yes, he is.

No, he does not think that Bad Bill and Monica was all about consensual sex. No, he doesn't want hard drugs legalized. Yes, he knows that we need to drastically upgrade our environmental restraints. Yes, he considers the death penalty an operational nightmare and would like to see it abolished.

Dinner-table chat resumed. No one asked me to justify my stand on Bill O'Reilly. Political issues were discussed—but I did not participate. The conversation was like-minded and self-congratulatory. My silence loomed large. I got glancing looks. Who's *this* guy? He's at *our* table. It's *our* spin zone. Why isn't he spinning along?

Spin this:

The No Spin Zone already exsists in your head. It's the clump of brain cells and developed native intelligence that allows you to detect lies and make precise value judgments. There's a collective No Spin Zone at work in America. It's a *non*-linked aggregate of *non*-like-minded people who love this country, distrust its leaders, and suspiciously assess most party lines and ideologies. These folks differ person to person. These folks straddle matters of Reason and Faith and take their politics issue by issue. These folks form a sizable but in no way majority consensus. Folks of all stripes. Non-spinners good, bad, and indifferent—along with some heavily disenfranchised and a small lunatic fringe. These folks are more likely to get Bill O'Reilly. Their bottom line is not shared opinion. Their assessment is that he's passionate and he means it, which is good enough for them.

The material No Spin Zone is a series of sound-stage sets. *The Factor* broadcasts chiefly out of the Fox News Channel in New York

City and frequently takes the show on the road. Sound sets look good on TV and jerry-rigged up close. You've got harsh lights, jammed-in equipment, and cable cords bunched on the floor. You've got a simple desk and chair for O'Reilly and his in-studio guests.

It's an incongruous setting for verbal battle and Bill O'Reilly's fierce and often contentious quest for the Truth. The media time clock is always running. Commercial breaks/the guest who bombs/ratings-fodder segments. There's no way to stop the clock and get in the final and wholly reflective assessment. There's no way to get O'Reilly at his absolute best.

Until this book.

You've read it. Buy another copy and give it to a friend. Lighten Big Bill's tax load.

He broils for the Truth. It drives his work ethic. He wants to be Martin Luther at Wittenberg. Honor him for it.

James Ellroy
Kansas City
7/8/01

Acknowledgments

All books are collaborative efforts because ideas and emotions do not occur in a vacuum. The following good people are all charter members of the No Spin Zone and helped me a lot: CHARLES FLOWERS, MAKEDA WUB-NEH, ERIC SIMONOFF, GERRY HOWARD, STEPHEN RUBIN, HEATHER FLAHERTY, EVAN BELL, DR. MON-ICA CROWLEY, LAURA INGRAHAM, CAROLE COOPER, RICHARD LEIBNER, ROGER AILES, CHET COLLIER, and JAMES ELLROY, the Sergeant at Arms of the No Spin Zone. Couldn't have done it without you guys!